BARBADOS
OUR ISLAND HOME

SIR ALEXANDER HOYOS

MACMILLAN
CARIBBEAN

First edition 1960 Reprinted three times
Second edition 1970 Reprinted four times
Third edition 1979 Reprinted three times
Fourth edition 1989
Published by
MACMILLAN EDUCATION LTD
London and Basingstoke
Companies and representatives throughout the world

ISBN 0–333–51612–5

13	12	11	10	9	8	7	6	5
06	05	04	03	02	01	00	99	

This book is printed on paper suitable for recycling and
made from fully managed and sustained forest sources.

Printed in Malaysia

By the same author:

Some Eminent Contemporaries
Two Hundred Years
The Story of the Progressive Movement
Our Common Heritage
Princess Margaret and the Memories of Our Past .
The Road to Responsible Government
The Rise of the West Indian Democracy
Background to Independence
*Barbados, Our Island Home
*Builders of Barbados
*Grantley Adams and the Social Revolution
*Barbados: A History from the Amerindians to Independence
*Barbados: The Visitors Guide
* The Quiet Revolutionary (Autobiography)
*Barbados Comes of Age
* Tom Adams: A Biography

(* Published by Macmillan)

FOREWORD TO THE FOURTH EDITION

I⊤ is a pleasant task to write a new foreword for the fourth edition of *Barbados, Our Island Home*. Readers will remember that it was once said 'Greater love hath no man than an author for his own works'. I do not claim to be an exception to this dictum.

I am indeed pleased to note the continuing success of *Barbados, Our Island Home*. The present edition follows the same plan as the previous ones. The first few chapters give a general description of Barbados, but they have had to be in some cases updated in order to show the substantial progress Barbados had made since the first, second and third editions of my little book made their appearance. The last chapter, moreover, has been expanded in order to record the changes in the island's development in recent times.

The plan of the book, however, remains substantially the same. The history of the island is interwoven with its geography and with the story of its plant and animal life. The present edition continues to be, therefore, an integrated narrative which seems to have been appreciated in the past by my readers, both adults and school children.

I owe a special debt of gratitude to those who helped not only to update the book but to provide photographs which made the narrative more useful and more attractive. At the risk of being invidious, I should perhaps make special mention of Mr. Wendell Kellman of the Prime Minister's Office, Mr. Pat Callender, Manager of Grantley Adams International Airport, Mrs. Margaret Hope and Mr. John Manning, head and deputy head respectively of the Government Information Office, Mr. Alistair Green and Mr. Michael Scantlebury of the Board of Tourism, Mr. Charles Alleyne and Sir Clyde Gollop of the Barbados Family Planning Association and Mr. Care Moore of the Central Bank of Barbados.

But I should perhaps be specially pleased to learn that teachers and pupils found the book of considerable assistance in their efforts to discover the charm and beauty of this island. Certainly, I should not omit mention of the Ministry of Education of the various administrations since 1960 when *Barbados, Our Island Home* made its first appearance. Without their support, the book could not have been established as a valuable aid in the programme of social studies.

Barbados, W.I., 1988   F.A.H.

CONTENTS

ACKNOWLEDGEMENTS

The publishers wish to acknowledge the help received from the following, who have supplied photographs on the pages mentioned:

All Souls College, Oxford, p. 116; the American Museum of Natural History, p. 32; the Barbados Museum and Historical Society, pp. 92, 106, 126; the Barbados Tourist Board, pp. 4, 12, 68; Hallam Gill, pp. 19, 20, 65, 101; R. N. Gill, p. 60; the Government Information Office, Barbados, pp. 9, 10, 15, 21, 137, 170, 190; Mr. Justice A. J. H. Hanschell, p. 142; Felix Kerr, pp. 53, 73; Mr. G. W. Lennox, p. 26; the Mansell Collection, p. 120; Thomas Nelson & Sons Ltd. (from West Indian Histories, Bk. III, by Captain E. W. Daniel) pp. 76, 83; Radio Times Hulton Picture Library, pp. 96, 112, 113; the Visual Aids Section, Department of Education, Barbados, pp. 44, 57, 69, 85, 102, 152, 173, 176, 182, 188; the West Indies Committee, p. 198; Zoological Society of London, p. 31. The photograph of Mr. Tom Adams on p. 206 is by courtesy of Lady Adams.

Dedication
for Gladys without whose love, patience
and industry I could not have made it.

Chapter 1

BARBADOS TO-DAY

BARBADOS is one of the most densely populated countries in the world. It is only a tiny island, with an area of one hundred and sixty-six square miles, yet it has more than 254,500 souls crowded together on its coral surface. There are about 1,500 persons to the square mile and you can imagine how grave a task it is to provide a living for all of its inhabitants.

The rate of annual increase in the island's population has fallen from the disturbing figures of former years to 2,281 in 1968. The main factor responsible for this has

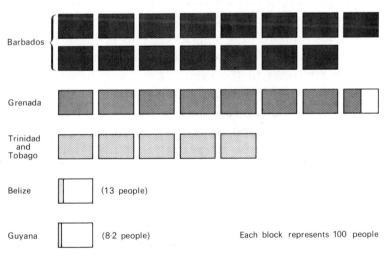

Number of People Per Square Mile in Some Caribbean Countries

been the dramatic fall in the birthrate from 33 per thousand in 1955 to 22 per thousand in 1968. In 1970 the figure recorded was 20·4 per thousand. In 1977 it was 17·6 per thousand and in 1987 it was 15·1 per thousand.

Undoubtedly, a major factor in this fall has been the work of the Barbados Family Planning Association. Started in 1954, under the leadership of Grace (later Lady) Adams and F. C. (later Sir Frank) Hutson, the Association has pursued a systematic campaign, with the financial and moral support of the Government. Net emigration, too, has had a significant effect in the control of the population. Although this has shown a marked decline over the decade, more males than females tend to leave Barbados to live abroad; this affects the number of marriages and lowers the birth rate on the island.

The above factors notwithstanding, the population of Barbados remains at a high level. This is due to the fact that there has been a substantial increase in the number of senior citizens in the island; the life span which was 45 years in 1937 is now 75 in 1988.

Thus, Barbados is still faced with the problem of providing economic opportunity for its growing population. But the people of the island do not easily admit defeat when difficulties beset them. Instead, they tackle them with the courage and energy that have been typical of the country throughout its history.

An Agricultural Community
The secret of the island's success lies not only in the

character of its people but in the natural advantages it possesses. In the first place, its coral limestone has become, by process of decay, a fertile loamy soil, with fine drainage and, since it is not a mountainous country, crops can be grown over most of its surface.

Thanks to its moderate altitude, there is no excessive rain, and no extensive swamps adversely affect the health of the people. Instead, the island as a whole receives a rainfall varying, from year to year, from 40 to 70 inches, which is quite satisfactory for agriculture in a tropical land. In addition, the gently rising terraces that take us to the fertile uplands make road transport in the island much easier than in most of the neighbouring territories. It is not surprising, therefore, that from its earliest days Barbados has had a more successful agriculture and a denser population than any other of the West Indian islands.

At one time 80 per cent of the island's limestone surface was planted with sugar cane or with 'sour grass' which is used for mulching and as fodder for cattle. The sugar industry was then one of the mainstays of the island's economy and was one of our largest employers. This is no longer the case owing to the price of sugar in the world market. Mechanical harvesting has been introduced to reduce our cost of production and as many as 17,000 workers are no longer employed in field and factory.

The thousands of peasants, who work on their own land have also been adversely affected by the present situation. Yet they continue to work on their small holdings, which were acquired by years of sweat, toil and thrift, and play

Cutting Sugar Cane, Our Staple Crop

their part, as in the past to maintain the island's national economy.

We are being advised by some experts in our midst that we should take account of the diversification strategy of the British firm, Tate and Lyle on the future of sugar. That company did not abandon the manufacture of sugar when the outlook of their central interest seemed gloomy. Instead, it moved into related fields such as food processing and distribution. 'It explored new production techniques for sugar and alternative uses for cane and other by-products of the firm's operations,' one Barbadian expert has written. 'The Company used its knowledge of sugar production and trade to find new avenues of profit.'

This is the discussion that is still proceeding in Barbados. Should the island adopt an approach similar to Tate and Lyle? Should we produce more sugar rather than less in order to earn the foreign exchange we badly need? Should we make use of the expertise we have acquired in the past in the sugar industry? These are some of the questions that are receiving the close attention of Government officials, the planting community and specialists in the field of sugar agriculture.

Meanwhile, there is general agreement that there has been increased production in Lisbon yam, Barbados cherries, black belly sheep, specialised furniture and selected areas of publishing.

From every planting of cane, four crops are produced in four successive years and, when the fields are rested from cane-growing in the fifth years, they are cultivated with such crops as sweet potatoes, and eddoes.

By this system of rotating the cane fields, Barbados is able to produce a quantity of these crops every year, though they are never sufficient to satisfy the food requirements of its people. Research is being undertaken to promote diversification in the island's agriculture. Improved sugar technology has increased the tonnage of cane by increasing the average yield of canes per acre, without extending the area planted with this crop. And our research programme has produced encouraging results in its experiments to increase the yields in such crops as corn and onions. This is a welcome addition to the quantity of vegetables and root crops that Barbados has already been producing for a number of years.

Fishing is an important source of the island's food supply and energetic efforts have been made to expand this industry. Beach shelters and new fish markets have been built. Improved methods of catching fish have been taken up by our hardy fishermen and the island's fishing fleet has been transformed, with powered vessels taking the place of the old sailing boats. With its mechanised fleet of several thousand launches, Barbados still holds a respectable place in the West Indies in regard to fishery development.

Thanks to the success of the United Nations Fishery Project, there has been a substantial increase in the catch of fish, and a new system of distribution has been introduced to ensure that as many persons as possible can purchase the fish they require. Good sales are made by those who go out in vans into the rural areas. In addition, fish is sold in considerable quantities at the markets in Fairchild Street, Eagle Hall and Six Cross Roads.

Industrial Development

In order to meet the situation facing Barbados, attention has been turned to two other spheres of economic activity: industrial development and tourism.

Much has been done in the field of industrial development since the Barbados Development Board, now renamed the Industrial Development Corporation, was established in 1957. The first modest efforts in the field included the manufacture of such articles as shirts, biscuits, margarine and soap. And the earliest pioneers to operate in an industrial park were those who manufactured furniture, concrete products and garments.

Since then, six parks have been established for the housing of various industries, at Grazettes, the Bridgetown Harbour, Wildey, Newton, Seawell and Six Cross Roads. The seventh park is contemplated for the north of the island in St. Peter. Some one hundred and sixty-eight new industries are now in operation and these directly employ more than 9,000 people. To these we must add those who obtain employment from these industries as cottage workers, bringing the total employed to more than 12,000.

The average rate of growth of manufacturing output is $6\frac{1}{2}$ per cent per annum. With the passing of each year since 1957, we have seen the expansion of our industrial activities, which have gradually become more varied, requiring wider knowledge and skills from our people. The early pioneering enterprises have been joined by factories that now turn out items ranging from building materials and metal products to drugs and electronic devices and agro-industries.

The Tourist Industry

It is undoubtedly the development of tourism that has had the biggest impact on the economy of the island. In 1987 it contributed 13% to the Gross Domestic Product of the country. It employed directly or indirectly approximately 20,000 persons which represented 24 per cent of the island's labour force of 85,000.

In 1987 this industry recorded 421,859 stay-over visitor arrivals. This was the largest number ever recorded in the island's history. Previously the highest number was received in 1979, when 370,916 arrivals were recorded. These visitors usually came from the United States of America (42%), United Kingdom (19%), Canada (15%) and the Caribbean (15%).

These were the figures for 1987. In the same year revenue from the industry was estimated at BDS.\$757·2 million. This was a significant improvement over the 1977 figure of BDS.\$221·5 million.

Barbados also benefits from a busy cruise ship industry. In 1987 the island recorded 228,778 cruise ship passenger arrivals. This was also the highest level of cruise traffic in the island's history.

The strengthening of the European currencies against the US dollar has stimulated traffic from Europe and the United Kingdom. Barbados has received its quota of visitors.

Barbados' reputation as an easily accessible destination with good quality accommodation and airline connections, as well as a good communications system and amiable population, has led to the island's continued success as a tourism destination.

The island has been successfully promoted and advertised in all the major markets through the Barbados Board

The Hilton Hotel

of Tourism. This agency, which was established in 1958, is responsible for the promotion of the island as a year round tourism destination. In 1987, the Board spent BDS.$7·6 million in the promotion of the island.

The wide range of accommodation from the luxury properties and villas, to the self catering apartments and small guest houses has made the island available to all income groups.

The problem of low summer occupancies has been addressed through the development of charter programmes designed to produce business in the slow periods. Programmes from the United Kingdom and Canada have,

The Terminal at Grantley Adams International Airport: gateway to Barbados

in large measure, helped to redress the problem of seasonality.

Not the least of the reasons why Barbados has made this rapid advance in the tourist industry is that it possesses certain natural advantages that are ideal for the trade both in summer and winter. There are the azure skies, white coral beaches and perennial sunshine. There are the transparent blue waters that surround the island and provide excellent sea-bathing. There are the miles of good road that connect almost all parts of the country, leading right up to the rolling hills of the north from where there is presented a panorama of interesting contours, rugged coast lines and pleasing landscapes.

Grantley Adams International Airport
The main gateway for the arrivals and departures of these tourists and the thousands of other people who enter and leave the island is the Grantley Adams International Airport. First started as Seawell International Airport in October 1938, it was renamed in 1976 after one of the island's national heroes.

During the more than 50 years of its existence, it has made remarkable progress. It now has a runway of 11,000 feet which enables it to accommodate the wide bodied aircraft of the present and the Concorde planes of the future. There is a parking space for 16 of the largest aircraft at any one time. But it is on record that as many as 77 aircraft of various types and sizes have been accommodated on its two parking aprons.

Not the least of the facilities offered by the airport are the plane connections with other parts of the Caribbean and the non-stop flights to New York, Toronto and Miami, Luxembourg, Zurich, Caracas and London. Such a development would not have been possible without the installation of the latest in radar technology and T Basis for guiding aircraft in to the land.

Without the modern facilities at the airport, Barbados would not have been able to reach the high level of tourism it now enjoys. It would not have seen the great increase in the volume of freight landed at, and exported from the airport.

Bridgetown from the Air, showing Liners in the New Harbour

A Bustling Port

Just over two decades ago, it was possible to say that the position of Barbados, as a centre of West Indian trade, was faced with a threat from Trinidad. The Barbadians, with characteristic enterprise, met what seemed to them to be a challenge. In spite of their limited resources, they constructed a deep water harbour at a cost of BDS.$28 million.

The new harbour, which is situated in Bridgetown, the capital and chief port of the island, is able to provide ocean-going liners with far better facilities than in the days when they anchored in Carlisle Bay. This, added to the facilities of Grantley Adams International Airport, has made it possible for Barbados to become one of the chief air and sea communication centres of the East and South Caribbean.

Carlisle Bay is no longer the centre it used to be. The ships that come from New York and New Orleans, from Halifax and Montreal, from Le Havre and Southampton, are no longer anchored in that open roadstead. All that you see in Carlisle Bay to-day is a few cruise ships from time to time, though the scene is enlivened by the sailing boats and yachts that travel up and down the Bay in search of pleasure and relaxation.

The great liners which once rode proudly at anchor in Carlisle Bay are now securely berthed along the piers of the Bridgetown Harbour. The great majority of the cruise ships now use the new harbour. It is true that the number of passengers travelling by sea has declined over the years.

It is interesting to note how history appears to be repeating itself. The little ships in the careenage take us back to a period when Barbados enjoyed to the full the advantage of its geographical position and gained a large measure of prosperity as a centre of inter-island trade. But this line cannot be pursued too far and one must resist a nostalgic yearning for the past.

This decline is undoubtedly due to the advantages of air travel and the acute competition that passenger ships have to meet from the airlines that use Grantley Adams International Airport. Yet it was accurately predicted that cruise ships would come to Barbados in increasing numbers and these would berth at the new Bridgetown Harbour.

The significance of the new harbour is that, in spite of competition from the airlines, it remains the island's main point of entry and exit for cargo. One of its chief services is the bulk shipment of sugar which is the major visible export of Barbados. In addition to this main activity, there is the export of the by-products of sugar, rum and molasses, the transhipment trade with the neighbouring islands and the import of the goods we need from various countries of the world.

But we must not forget the quaint little inner harbour or careenage which is situated right in the heart of the City of Bridgetown. The Bridgetown Harbour now provides a shallow draft pier for intra-Caribbean traffic. And the careenage, while remaining a picturesque feature of the City, will not longer be the busy centre it used to be.

It is clear that a good town and country planning programme would not permit the congestion that a bustling careenage is certain to create and thus aggravate the growing traffic problems in the heart of the city. To prevent such a situation from developing, the Bridgetown Harbour has been extended and improved and facilities have been introduced to provide adequately for modern container traffic.

A Sense of Community
In view of its activities, it is not surprising that Bridgetown, though a small town by world standards, is regarded

The Bustle of Life in Bridgetown

by the Barbadian as a great metropolis. Indeed, to him it is the hub of the universe. There he hears the latest news and finds opportunities for employment. There he knows he is in touch with the remoter parts of the globe to which he can travel, if he has the money, by the most up to date methods of transport. There he feels the throb of a great little city which is still significant because it lies on the important trade routes of the world.

The feeling of pride in the island is shared by all classes

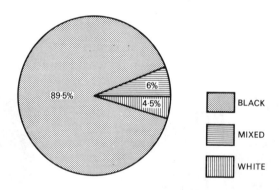

Racial Groups in the Population of Barbados

of the community. The strong patriotism of the islanders animates all sections of the population, white, black and mixed. This is perhaps the chief characteristic that gives Barbados a personality that is different from that of any other mixed community in the Caribbean.

Although the whites in the island number under 5 per cent of the population, this is the highest proportion of people of European descent in any of the Commonwealth

Caribbean territories. They no longer control the politics of the island, as in the days when they formed a powerful oligarchy. But, in spite of the chances and changes of Barbadian history, they still own much of the island's wealth and play a leading role in the economic life of the community.

With the advance of democracy, political power has passed into the hands of the majority, the black and mixed people of Barbados. The descendants of the slaves now govern the island and occupy the high places once held by their masters. Yet, though the cause of progress and reform has made rapid strides during the past two decades, it is remarkable how restrained the majority has been in the exercise of the power it now enjoys. The recent history of our island home could have been quite different, if bitterness and resentment had taken the place of tolerance and goodwill. As it was, the island advanced in a spirit of give and take, and thus the best elements of the Barbadian character have been preserved.

By a happy combination of circumstances, Barbados to-day still boasts the financial security of its former days. In spite of differences between capital and labour, industrial life proceeds with comparative smoothness and harmony. Parliamentary government continues to flourish as in the early days and, notwithstanding the sharp differences inevitable in party politics, the island enjoys a large measure of political stability.

Such a fortunate state of affairs has been possible because Barbadians of whatever race, colour or class, feel that they are first and foremost, citizens of their island home. Their long record of achievements gives them a tradition of which they are justly proud. It gives them a sense of oneness, a feeling that they belong not to different warring sections but to a single community. Proud of the heritage of the past, the various sections of the island work together, as they have done for many years, to maintain the unique position Barbados has long held in the British Caribbean.

Further Reading

Barbados Airport Manual, 1986.
Barbados Economic Survey 1987.
The Future of Tourism in the Eastern Caribbean
    by H. Zinder and Associates Inc., May 1969.
The New Bajan Magazine October 1988.

Chapter 2

THE KISS OF THE SUN

As you move away from the city of Bridgetown, you soon realise that Barbados is far more pleasant than you may have thought at first. The heat and bustle of the city give place to the cool trade winds and the leisurely pace of life in the rural areas. The noise and confusion of the town are forgotten in the serenity of the countryside. The congestion of the city's buildings and streets are atoned for by the beauty of the winding country lanes and the colours of trees, shrubs and flowers.

Even in the countryside you will receive the clear impression that Barbados is a densely populated land. Wherever you go, you will see the long rows of carefully arranged fields broken at regular intervals of about a mile by the houses of a crowded village; while plantation buildings can be observed quite frequently since they are only partly hidden when the canes are in full bloom. But, if you are observant, you will notice that the villages and farm houses are usually situated on land that is of no agricultural value for the simple reason that the island cannot afford to give up good soil for building purposes.

Barbados has been rightly described as a well-cultivated garden. Shady trees grow along the sides of the roads, in plantation yards and near dwelling houses. One of the most gracious of these is the mahogany tree which is a great blessing because it protects us from the rays of the

Mahogany Trees at the Lodge School

blistering sun. It sheds its leaves in the earlier part of the year and these take on yellow, brown and reddish tints just before falling to the ground. The fruit of the mahogany look like large pear-shaped capsules and its wood is in great demand for making furniture.

Also providing welcome shade from the hot sun is the tamarind. This is a tall tree with many branches, thick with leaves and clustered with pleasant-smelling flowers. Its fruit, which has an acid yet attractive taste, is very popular in the island and is also being exported in increasing quantities. Do you know that the Barbadian tamarinds are much sought after by people outside the island and that they are used in the manufacture of Lea and Perrin's Worcester Sauce, sold all over the world?

The evergreen does not grow to a great height, but its branches are thick and wide-spreading. It is usually planted near dwelling houses or in plantation yards where horses and other animals can be tethered beneath its protecting shade. Years ago, when there were white indentured servants and African slaves in the island, they used to gather under the evergreen tree for their midday rest instead of returning to their humble shacks.

Woman's tongue, which was introduced into the island in the nineteenth century, is noted for its numerous, pale-

Evergreen Trees in the 'Lower Green', Bridgetown

brown pods within which the loose seeds rattle noisily,
when shaken by the wind. This tree has been given its
name by uncharitable people who say that the rattling
pods sound like chattering females. The wood from
woman's tongue and from the fustic tree help to make
the wheels of the curious little donkey carts which you
still see travelling up and down the island.

The casuarina is also a comparative newcomer to the

Casuarina Trees

island and has quickly adapted itself to local conditions. With its extensive root system, it has proved itself a fast-growing tree that is not affected by long periods of drought. Its bark is rugged, its branches slender and it towers above other trees like graceful spires, sometimes growing as high as one hundred and fifty feet. It is the tree that appeals most to the imagination of the Barbadian poet and Mr. Frank Collymore has written a poem which is quoted below and which you should perhaps commit to your memory.

> We walk slowly beneath the casuarinas
>   Our feet make no sound on the thick pile spread
> Beneath the trees' shade: all is silent:
>   We walk with muted footsteps and no word is said.
> Overhead the casuarinas strain upwards to the sky
>   Their dull green plumage vainly poised for flight;
> Around us everything is strange and still
>   And all is filled with unreal light:
> We might be walking along a timeless floor
>   Of a sea where desolate tides forever creep
> Or roaming along the secret paths
>   That wind among the twilight plains of sleep.

Variety and Colour

In addition to the shade-giving trees I have just mentioned, there are many flowering trees that give variety and colour to the Barbadian scene. One of these is the flamboyant. It has been acclaimed by some botanists as 'the most beautiful tree in the world'. The red flamboyant has pale green leaves and these are surmounted by bright scarlet flowers. When it is in flower, it is a delightful mass of bloom, surpassed by no other ornamental tree in the tropics. The yellow flamboyant is also a very attractive tree, with open flowers and spreading, bright yellow petals.

The frangipani, which flourishes even in dry soil, grows in two closely-related species, white and red. The white frangipani, more frequently known as the jasmine tree, bears its leaves in bunches on twigs that are forked. When the dry season begins, the leaves fall off and their place is taken by heavily-scented flowers.

The Red Frangipani

Have you ever heard how the frangipani got its name? It was once the name of an Italian who invented a rare and delicate perfume which was very popular among the high-born ladies of Europe. It was a perfume no one could mistake and for many years it reigned supreme among all other perfumes. And when the first settlers came to Barbados and other lands in the Caribbean, they were so fascinated by the scent of the frangipani that they at once gave it the name by which it is now known.

The scarlet cordia grows in the island as it must have grown from time immemorial. It is a common sight in gardens. An evergreen of medium height, it is clothed in large, stiff leaves and bears flowers abundantly all around the year. The brilliance of its flowers is a spectacle that never fails to delight the lover of the beautiful.

Equally prodigal with its flowers is the black willow, a small evergreen tree. Its leaves are smooth and dark-green on one side, with a rough, grey surface on the other, and its flowers, like those of the white willow, bloom in every month of the year. Both the black and the white willow are great favourites with those who like to beautify their surroundings.

Equal favourites are the cassias, small, graceful trees, which grow in several varieties, the purging cassia, the horse cassia and the pink cassia. They each produce flowers of different colours, bright yellow, pink and pink-rose. Though their bloom lasts a comparatively short time, they are still very welcome because they decorate gardens, estate yards and roadsides during certain months of the year with short-lived but delightful blossoms.

To these ornamental trees may be added the flowering shrubs and climbers that beautify the island. The pink of the coralita, the purple and magenta of the bougain-villea, the red and yellow of the Barbados Pride and the bright scarlet of the poinsettia or Star of Bethlehem help to give the island a setting of varied colour and rare beauty.

Fruit Trees

The fruit trees which grow in the island in considerable numbers may be divided into three kinds. The first are called 'deciduous' because they drop all their leaves once a year. In this class are the hog and Chili plum trees which produce their leaves, flowers and fruit at the same period of the year. It would be difficult to find fruit more delicious than hog and Chili plums. The golden apple bears an abundant harvest of yellow fruit which looks, at times, like a cascade of gold. Other deciduous fruit trees are the sugar apple, the sour sop and the custard apple and children regard themselves as very lucky if they have any such tree growing in their backyards.

The second class of fruit trees are 'evergreens'. They are called evergreens because they keep most of their leaves throughout the year. A fine example of this type is the breadfruit tree which was introduced into the West Indies in 1793 by the famous Captain Bligh of the *Bounty*. It bears large, shiny leaves and its fruit is very widely used as a vegetable. Other evergreen fruit trees are the mango,

A Breadfruit Tree

avocado pear, citrus, mammee apple and the cashew. They all flower at about the same time and bear their fruit shortly after the rains begin to fall.

The third class of fruit trees are also evergreens. But these are very different from the ones I have just mentioned because their flowering and fruiting take place at irregular periods. Sometimes they produce no crop at all. Sometimes they produce more than one crop a year. In this class are the cherry, dunk, gooseberry, guava, akee, sapodilla and star apple.

Barbados is indeed an island of which the utmost has been made. But the Barbadian soil and climate are not really suited for the cultivation of fruit trees on a large scale. Our soil is not of volcanic origin, as is the case with other West Indian islands which produce fruit in abundance. Being made from the underlying limestone, it contains too much lime and this prevents our fruit trees from bearing well. Moreover, these trees do not get enough water because our rainfall is not sufficient for this purpose.

Such fruit trees as grapefruit, orange, sapodilla, cashew and guava have to be planted in places that are shady and moist and protected from the trade winds. It is not surprising, therefore, that the fruit grown in Barbados is far from adequate for the needs of its population and consequently not sufficient to develop an export trade.

Thus it is that sugar has continued to be the staple crop of the island. Attempts have been made from time to time to revive cotton as a major crop. But when the U.S.A. began the cultivation of cotton on a large scale in the nineteenth century, Barbados was forced to give even more attention to sugar as its principal product.

A Garden Island

When you walk or drive through the countryside, you will enjoy the many charms with which nature has endowed the island. You will be fascinated by the many tints and hues of the hibiscus, the white, pink and mauve of the queen of flowers, the cobalt-blue of the morning glory and the rich crimson of the sweet william. You will see the sun shining on green cane fields and feel the rustling of the wind as it whistles through the waving cane arrows. At night, when the moon is shining in all its brilliance, you will see the tall, majestic cabbage palms waving their branches serenely from side to side and you may hear the strange music the trade winds seem to play, with the foliage of the casuarinas as their delicate instrument. And always you will savour the fragrance of the many scents that come from the trees, the shrubs and the flowers that give the island the appearance of a trim well-kept garden. Perhaps you may then be moved to agree with the poet that we have special reasons to be grateful for the natural beauty of our island home.

> *The kiss of the sun for pardon,*
> *The song of the birds for mirth,*
> *One is nearer God's heart in a garden*
> *Than anywhere else on earth.*
>
> *The glow of the dawn for glory,*
> *The hush of the night for peace:*
> *In the garden at eve, says the story,*
> *God walks and His smile brings release.*

Further Reading

Some Aspects of the Flora of Barbados by F. Hardy.
Flowering Trees of the Caribbean by W. White.
Flowers of the Caribbean by G. W. Lennox and S. A. Seddon.

Chapter 3

OUR ANIMAL KINGDOM

LET us now have a look at the animal kingdom of Barbados. You must, first of all, bear in mind that the island is not a place like Guyana where large primeval forests have preserved the wild life of that country for countless years. In that South American land you will find species of plants and animals that have survived in remote areas, almost undisturbed by men for thousands of years.

In Barbados, it has been entirely different. In a small island like ours, with a teeming population, almost every available spot has been used for man's habitation or for the growing of his crops. This is why various species of plant and animal life, which might have spread here from the South American continent, have been unable to establish themselves in the island since its occupation by man.

Mammals and Reptiles

Domestic animals like sheep and goats are scattered in considerable numbers throughout the island. They are extremely useful animals but their constant grazing has destroyed all the places where any kind of strange mammals and reptiles might have been able to live.

Dogs and cats are other domestic animals brought to the island by the first settlers and established here ever since. In other islands of the West Indies, dogs and cats are said to have been responsible for the destruction of certain reptiles, but this has not been the case in Barbados. In this island there are only two species of snakes, both harmless, and it has never been necessary for man to protect himself against them. The cat has certainly been useful in killing one of the most common pests in the island, the household mouse.

The lizards, which dart hither and thither in the trees and less frequently in houses, are the sort of reptiles we should cherish. For, while they are in no way as interesting as those that are to be found in Guyana and Belize, they do valuable work as scavengers, eating the insect pests known as house flies, of which we shall tell you more in a moment. Lizards are found in seven different species in this island.

The green monkey lives a somewhat precarious life in the island. His existence is threatened by two things. First, he is a destructive animal, attacking fruit trees and birds, and he is therefore shot at as soon as he shows his face in certain areas. Moreover, the few woodlands of the island are constantly growing fewer and it is becoming increasingly difficult for the monkey to find somewhere to live. This may also be the reason why the Barbadian parrot, found here by the early settlers, is now extinct.

Perhaps the most destructive of all the imported animals is the mongoose. Introduced into the island in the late nineteenth century, it did the island a great service, at first, by destroying many of the rats which did heavy damage to the sugar industry. In other islands of the West Indies it was imported to kill snakes but in Barbados its task was to eradicate the rats.

Now the rats have been brought under a measure of control — though they are still a problem on many of the island's estates — the mongoose has turned its attention to other animals. It has worked havoc among mammals, reptiles and birds. This has been lamented by the field naturalist. But to the practical Barbadian it was a graver problem when young pigs, lambs and calves were killed by this creature. It is not surprising that in 1904 the Barbados Legislature passed an Act providing for the destruction of the mongoose. But he still lives on and can often be seen scurrying from garden to garden in the town or from one cane field to another in country districts.

Other imported creatures include the giant toad or bull

A Common American Toad

frog which came to Barbados from South America and adapted itself quite easily to the conditions in this island. The rabbit was also imported and is still flourishing, but the common hare, another creature which was imported into the island, is rapidly being exterminated by over-enthusiastic sportsmen.

Most visitors are particularly struck by the whistling frog because he usually keeps them up at night until they get used to his piercing notes. The adult is one inch long, the female being larger than the male. It is brown and yellow in colour, with a broad band of muddy yellow over

A Whistling Frog

its back, and its digits end in swollen discs. Its young
do not go through the tadpole stage, but after ten days
a small frog emerges from the jelly.

Resident Birds

You have seen that Barbados has few of the native mammals that can be found in other tropical lands. We also
have to admit that its birds are in no way as varied or as
plentiful as those of Trinidad or Guyana.

Still, there is a number of different species of birds that
you will find of great interest. If you go out of doors and
have a good look around you, you will find some eighteen
kinds of resident birds in the island. One of the best ways
you can spend your leisure time is to try and identify the
birds of the island.

You will see one of the commonest birds in the island,
the sugar bird or yellow breast. It is very fond of fruit
juices and nectar and is, therefore, frequently seen flying
around fruit trees and flowers. Its upper body is of a
sooty grey, but what makes it conspicuous is its yellow
breast, its white eyestripe and its bill brightened with a

A Yellow Breast or Sugar Bird

coral-red patch. You will also see the wood dove which is larger and more common than the ground dove. It is a thick-set little bird and its colours are nicely arranged. The upper part of its body is a greyish brown and the rest of it is varied with such colours as black, white and cinnamon.

An interesting newcomer to the island — it arrived early in the present century — is the grass finch. It has adjusted itself to conditions in Barbados more easily than any other foreign bird. Indeed, it not only decided to stay in the island but increased and multiplied to such an extent that it can now be seen in large numbers. It is a small, brown bird, with a brilliant yellow breast, and lives in grassfields and savannahs.

A very pretty bird is the canary or the golden warbler. It is a little mass of yellow, which sometimes takes on a golden and greenish tint. Here and there on its little body you will notice streaks of dark chestnut. In other countries you would see its nest neatly built in a bush or a tree, and schoolboys are often tempted to disturb its spotted eggs. But in Barbados the golden warbler is rarely seen, probably because it is the special target of that destructive parasite, the cowbird.

The cowbird came to the island in 1899. It came from South America and can be seen in most of the Leeward Islands. It is easily confused with the blackbird — the female is brown in colour and the male is a glossy black. The cowbird is not a welcome resident in the island because it threatens the existence of other birds, especially small ones, like the golden warbler. It lays its eggs in the nests of other birds and the result is that small birds have little chance of keeping their eggs undisturbed and hatching others of their kind. The cowbird is spreading throughout the West Indies and this means that little birds may suffer the same fate as they do in Barbados.

And what about the parakeet? It is called a love-bird and its colour is a delightful green. It is a small bird and is sometimes seen flying over various parts of the island and chattering excitedly with its neighbours. It was once held in captivity but has since escaped and seems to enjoy its freedom.

Birds of Passage

Although there are not many resident birds in the island, Barbados is fortunate to have quite a large number of visitors or birds of passage.

One of the most frequent visitors to the island is the frigate or man-o'-war bird. You probably know it better as the cobbler. It is mainly black, with glosses of green and purple, orange and red. You usually see it flying high above the sea, on outstretched wings. It will frequently swoop down to catch something on the surface of the water and then it will fly up again just as swiftly as it came down.

The frigate bird is not the only sea-bird that visits Barbados. There is the brown pelican which is a fine sight when it is flying in the air. These birds fly in small flocks. They advance in single file, making their way with a few wing-beats, followed by a long glide, and keep together in perfect formation. Unfortunately, they are not seen very frequently in Barbados. Some of them tried to settle on the St. Lawrence coast in 1957 but they were killed or driven away by some uninformed persons who imagined, curiously enough, that they would bring malaria to the island.

Again, there is the sea gull, another sea-bird, which is usually seen off the coast during the hurricane season. It is better known as the laughing gull. Its feathers are white, its mantle and wings grey and its feet a pale pink. The laughing gull breeds in the Grenadines and Tobago, where its young are more likely to be undisturbed than in the more crowded islands of the West Indies.

A Frigate-bird or Man-o'-War

But most of the birds that visit us are shore birds. Among these are the grey plover, noted for its black breast, grey back and black and white tail, the snipe, with its long, straight bill, and the sandpiper, with its yellow feet and slender bill.

The favourite with some people is the Christmas bird. It is beautifully coloured in orange and black and yellow and its singing is very pleasant, but although we enjoy the beauty of its colours we never hear its song in the West Indies. For the Christmas bird will only sing in temperate climates when spring has ended the long dreary months of winter. That is a pity because it is really a warbler and its notes are very musical.

Barbados is lucky in one respect. It seems that, because of its position as the most easterly of the West Indies, it is visited by birds that come a long distance across the Atlantic Ocean. Some of these visitors have been the Greenland wheatear, the alpine swift, the wood sandpiper, the ruff and the black-headed gull. These all come from Europe and Africa and land in Barbados as the nearest port of call after their long journey. Perhaps they then go on to visit other islands in the Caribbean but no one seems to have observed them.

Insects

The house-fly is an insect that can do a great deal of damage. You usually find it in the kitchen or wherever food is stored and it deposits germs on the things you have to eat. The house-fly is very dangerous because it carries germs and transfers them to man through his food. These germs are picked up when the house-fly feeds on decaying matter such as dead animals and human faeces. By infecting you with those germs, it can give you such diseases as typhoid and dysentery.

The cabbage white butterfly, which has large, white, flapping wings, is another common insect pest. It is a great source of worry to those who grow cabbages, since it lays its eggs on this plant and these produce the larvae which grow as caterpillars from one-tenth of an inch to two inches in three weeks. They grow from the food they get from the cabbage and this shows you how much damage they can do in a short time. The adult lays about fifty eggs in one clutch and the caterpillars from these can completely destroy a cabbage head.

There are three kinds of mosquitoes which have been found in Barbados, the common mosquito, the malaria mosquito and the yellow fever mosquito. The germs from the first can cause elephantiasis, a disease more commonly known as Barbados leg. These germs infect and block the tissues of the legs and cause them to swell. Fortunately, the malaria mosquito has not been found here since 1927 and more recently the World Health Organisation carried out a campaign to eradicate the yellow fever mosquito. It is the female that is dangerous. It punctures the skin in order to suck blood from our veins, and while it is feeding it pours germs into the blood stream, where they rapidly grow and multiply.

The bee, on the other hand, is a useful insect because

it produces honey. It also flies from flower to flower, in search of nectar, and fertilises the female by transferring to it the pollen of the male. There are three kinds of this insect, the queen bee — there is only one in a whole hive and it lays the eggs — the drone bee and the worker bee. The drone is lazy but the worker is very industrious. They live in a highly-organized society and they can communicate with each other through some means which is not known. They organize themselves in groups to carry out such activities as cleaning hives, looking after the young and finding food.

There are other insects on which we could go on speaking to you for a long time, but a few words must suffice. Among those you will notice are the ants, which can be quite a nuisance in home and garden, the wood ants, which are termites and destroy trees and houses, the cockroaches, which have a ravenous appetite for such things as human food and clothing, and the grasshopper, which makes curious noises and is capable of leaping remarkable distances.

The earthworm is not an insect but we want to make mention of it here because it is extremely useful to man. It is an invertebrate or an animal without a backbone. It lives in the earth, burrowing deep down and making the soil porous. As a result, water and air can circulate in the soil and the roots of plants can penetrate the earth more easily. The earthworm also brings up rich soil from below to the surface. It is estimated that, if an acre of soil is well-populated with earthworms, the latter will bring twenty-eight tons of rich fertile soil from below to the surface of the earth. Moreover, the earthworm digs right down to the coral rock, establishing a passage through which water and air can reach the coral and dissolve it, thus forming new soil.

In the Waters Around Us

Fish of many kinds are to be found in large quantities in the waters around us. The most important of them all is perhaps the flying fish which is caught in great schools off the coast. The catch of flying fish will vary from year to year as it depends on the movement of the ocean currents, particularly the north and south equatorial currents. These fish are found plentifully in water temperatures of 78° to 82° Fahrenheit. When the main stream of the currents passes close to the island, flying fish are plentiful. But when the stream is more than twelve miles distant from the island, these fish are then beyond the range of most of the fishing boats. The gill net is now used to catch flying fish — these push their heads into the net and are then unable to extricate themselves — and this method has trebled the catch of fish in recent years.

Second in importance to the flying fish is the green dolphin, which is also caught in large quantities. This fish is a curious combination of green, yellow and blue, with dark spots, and the fascinating thing about it is that it seems to be constantly changing from one colour phase to another. Other fish which make popular dishes are the cavalla, which is bright green or blue-green on the back

A Flying Fish and a Green Dolphin

and upper sides, the Spanish mackerel, a blend of blue, green and silver, and the delicate ale wife, which is known to the Barbadian as old wife.

The wahoo, locally known as king fish, and the barracuda are also found abundantly in the waters around us. The barracuda grows as long as three feet and its flesh makes quite an appetizing dish. Some regard it as a dangerous fish to meet in the sea and it has been called the pike of the ocean, but it is not ferocious enough to deserve this name. It is more than usually curious and circles around those who venture far out into the sea. It retreats if you move towards it and will only attack at night if you make a sudden splash or movement.

We should say something about the small freshwater fishes called 'millions' which play a useful part in protecting the health of the island. Indeed, Barbados has received a great deal of credit through the work of these fish. They have been exported to Jamaica, St. Kitts, Nevis, St. Vincent and St. Lucia where they feed on the larvae which, if left undisturbed, grow into mosquitoes that can infect the people they bite with malaria fever. It is due both to our climate and to the work of these 'millions' that Barbados is happily free from the dreaded malaria fever.

You must have seen or heard of the pilot fish. It swims near ships to get whatever food may be thrown overboard. More often, it accompanies sharks to feed on what these monsters may leave after a meal. Indeed, you cannot think of a pilot fish without at once thinking of a shark.

The shark you will find most frequently in Barbadian waters is the puppy shark, which is quite harmless. But at times you will find more formidable specimens like the brown shark, the Blue Peter and the tiger shark. The last is a particularly delicious fish — most people think it is even more palatable than the green dolphin. Perhaps I should reassure you by saying that these monsters are caught by fishermen many miles off our coast. To catch them the fishermen use a heavy line, with a single hook, baited with flying fish.

You may be amused to hear about the sleeping shark. It prowls about at night and during the day it is so exhausted that it sleeps in the waters off Harrison Point and Stroud's Bay in St. Lucy. The fishermen set out in a boat to the area, where these sharks doze all day, dive down gently into the water, slip a noose around their tails and then just as gently return to their boats, without waking them from their slumbers. Once they reach the safety of their boats, the fishermen then haul up the sharks and a brisk battle takes place until the giant fish are clubbed to death.

When the flying fish season comes to an end — it starts in October and finishes in July — the fishermen turn their attention to other fish. Among these are the four important groups, bream, grouper, snapper and amber jack. The snapper lives in depths of about thirty-five to eighty fathoms. The bream and amber jack prefer deeper waters that go down as far as one hundred and twenty fathoms. The bream is a bright red scaled fish, with dark blue bulging eyes and white flesh, and makes a most pleasant dish. The snapper is of a light pink colour, with blue eyes surrounded by yellow iris, while the amber jack is silvery coloured, with greenish tints along the upper portion of its back. The grouper family varies in colour with such specimens as the black grouper, the brown grouper and the red grouper.

In the tuna family is the yellow-finned tuna, locally called the albacore. It is often caught in sizes up to two hundred pounds. In February, 1958, an exceptionally good specimen was caught, weighing five hundred and six pounds — which exceeds the world record, but was unfortunately not registered as such. The bonito group is often seen in five species and these are also caught in reasonably large numbers.

The Barbados sea egg is the only thing of its kind you will find in all the West Indies. It is a sea urchin and at certain times of the year you will see men and women on the beach preparing it for the local market. The roes of the sea urchin are extracted from the inner walls of the shell, collected in some numbers and then packed in a prepared shell. The finished product is then marketed under the local name of sea egg.

As a rule, you can swim about in the sea, safe from any danger, and enjoy watching the many fishes that paddle hither and thither, inspecting everything they see with

Preparing Sea Eggs for Market at Silver Sands, Christ Church

much curiosity. And there will be many things to delight your eyes — the rock hind, with the small, dark spots of its body, the rich colours of the yellow tail snapper, the lively hues of the angel fish and the black, orange and brimstone of the yellow coat chub.

Further Reading

Birds of the West Indies by James Bond.
Some Observations on the Birds of Barbados by F. C. K. Anderson.
The Natural History of Barbados by Griffith Hughes.
Nature Preservation in the Caribbean by J. H. Westermann.

Chapter 4

THE BEGINNING OF THE ISLAND

IN the first three chapters of this book we have tried to give you an idea of what Barbados looks like to-day. I have provided a brief outline of its various activities and enterprises, of the different sections of the Barbados population and of the plant and animal life of the island.

Have you ever wondered how Barbados came to be the kind of place it is to-day? How it was formed as an island and assumed its present size and shape? How it became a fertile spot, covered with plants and vegetation? Have you ever asked yourself how its soil and climate determined the sort of crops the island could grow? What attracted its animals and birds to make their abode in the country? How it became a multi-racial community of white, black and mixed people? What circumstances gave birth to its present system of government?

These are only some of the many questions you have every right to ask, if you want to understand why Barbados has its present character. In this chapter and in the chapters that follow it, I shall tell you the story of the origin and development of the island. It is a narrative that should interest you because it will show you how the forces of nature work in the world around us. It will indicate how Barbadians have reacted to the environment in which they had to live and move. It will demonstrate the triumph of the Barbadian character over circumstances that have at times threatened the welfare of the island.

If you could look through the ocean, you would see a system of mountains beneath the sea, linking Puerto Rico with Haiti and Cuba, with Jamaica and Central America. To the south of that mountain range you would see a line of volcanic peaks, stretching from the Virgin Islands through Nevis, St. Kitts, Montserrat, Dominica, St. Lucia and St. Vincent down to Grenada. A hundred miles to the east of that arc stands Barbados, an island that is completely different from the others mentioned above because of its position, its comparatively flat surface and its coral formation.

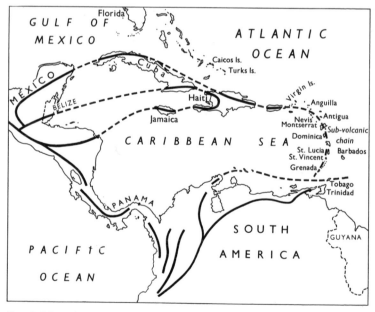

Sketch Map of the Mountain Ranges in the Area

The Formation of Barbados

Now let us go right back to the very beginning of our history. Many, many years ago, if we had been alive at the time, we would not have recognised the Caribbean region. Its geography was entirely different from what it is to-day. There were no islands, as we know them now, stretching in an arc from the Gulf of Mexico to the northern part of South America. The spot we call Barbados was covered by shallow water and nearby was a large tract of land with mountain ranges and swift-flowing rivers.

That land mass was the continent of South America, which stretched much farther north than it does to-day and was, in fact, quite close to Barbados. From the mountains of South America, rivers flowed down to the sea, bringing with them large quantities of mud, sand and grit which settled on the ocean floor in the area now occupied by Barbados and formed the foundation of the island. This foundation is made up of sandstone strata which are the soft rocks found in the Scotland District on the east coast of the island.

It is in the Scotland District, so called by our ancestors because it reminded them of the Scottish Highlands, that we can see the beds of sandstone and clays which were formed at the very beginning of our history. The next time you visit that area you should pay careful attention to the formulations you will see, for they go right back to the very birth of Barbados.

While the foundation of the island was being formed, a strange and awful thing began to happen to all the land in the Caribbean. It started to sink into the ocean, taking the future Barbados along with it. This sinking went on for a long time and carried the island deep down below the level of the sea. Then there came a time when there was almost no land at all to be seen above the surface of the ocean. Our island home became a part of the ocean bed, having sunk to a depth of more than a mile beneath the waters of the Caribbean.

But the ocean had not ceased to perform its miracles in the Caribbean. The building of Barbados continued under a great depth of water and the second layer of the island was formed by the debris from vast mud volcanoes, probably caused by high gas pressure in the underlying Scotland beds. This section or stratum of the island is now known as Joe's River Mud and consists of a dead, black, oil-soaked clay.

The forces of nature still went on with their task of forming Barbados, now working with the skeletons of tiny sea creatures that were lying on the floor of the sea. The third layer of the island was formed by these oceanic deposits which were laid as a continuous sheet that covered the first beds of sandstones and clays and the stratum of Joe's River Mud.

These oceanic deposits can be seen to-day in certain parts of the island — in the Scotland Hills and on the sides of Mount Hillaby, near Mount Misery, Canefield and Springvale. You should go on an expedition some day and look at those exposed beds. You will find them in the higher areas of the island and at lower levels near the sea. Those who are learned in the science of geology tell us that this part of the island was built deep down on the ocean floor because these deposits resemble the ones that are being formed at the present time far down beneath the surface of the water in the Indian and Pacific Oceans.

The building of the second and third layers of the island took up a long period in the ancient history of Barbados. Then there were fearful happenings in the waters that now surround us. Volcanoes erupted in the mass of land beneath the sea and the ocean floor was greatly disturbed. In the upheaval which then took place in the area, the inner arc of the Lesser Antilles began to move upwards from its resting place deep down on the ocean floor. It is probable that masses of lava, escaping from the volcanoes, flowed into the underlying rocks of these islands and began to force them upwards.

Emergence from the Sea

Thus it was that these submerged lands of the Caribbean made their ascent through the ocean. Eventually they appeared above the sea and to-day we know them as volcanic islands because they are made of ash and lava. Barbados, however, was not affected by the submarine eruptions. The uplift of the island from its resting place on the ocean floor was caused by the pressure from its sides. The first pressure, which came from the south-west, buckled it slightly and raised the northern half of the island.

Gradually Barbados established itself as an island, cut

off from all other lands by the ocean. It consisted of a
foundation of soft rocks and was covered over a large part
of its surface by a layer of coral limestone. That is why
it is called a coral island, while many of the other islands
in the West Indies are of volcanic origin.

The coral rock, in which Barbados was then encased,
was the fourth and last deposit in the building of the
island and had been formed over a large platform just
under the sea. This part of the island was built by strange
little animals called coral polyps. These tiny animals
played a part in the building of Barbados because, by a
miracle of nature, they were able to extract lime from sea
water and deposit it as limestone on the surface of their
bodies. And when they died their limestone-covered
skeletons in countless numbers went to form a portion
of the island.

If you are fond of diving in the sea, you should inspect
the coral reefs around the island. There you will see the
beautiful coral gardens of green and tan, orange and
purple. There you will see the little land builders, actually
alive and in the process of building coral reefs, just as
they helped to build Barbados over a long period of time.

At first Barbados did not have the size and shape we
know to-day, since only a part of it had emerged from the
sea. Then, a short time afterwards, another pressure began
to be exerted on the island, this time from the south and,
as a result, the Christ Church ridge came out of the sea.
At first this southern portion was separated from the rest
of the island by the sea, which then flowed over the site
of what is now called the St. George's Valley.

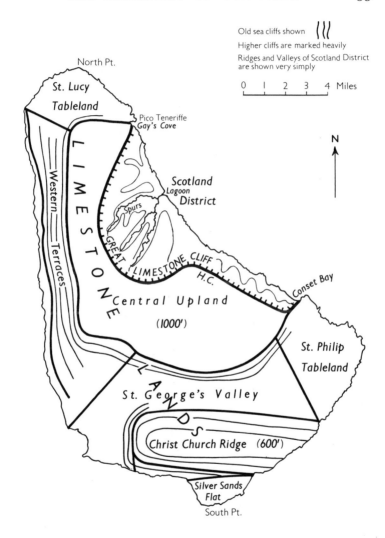

Old sea cliffs shown {{{

Higher cliffs are marked heavily

Ridges and Valleys of Scotland District
are shown very simply

0   1   2   3   4   Miles

N

North Pt.

St. Lucy
Tableland

Pico Teneriffe
Gay's Cove

L I M E S T O N E

Western ——— Terraces

Scotland
Lagoon
District

Spurs

GREAT

LIMESTONE CLIFF

H.C.

Conset Bay

Central Upland

(1000')

St. Philip

Tableland

St. George's Valley

Christ Church Ridge   (600')

Silver Sands
Flat

South Pt.

Sketch Map of the Relief Regions of Barbados

In course of time, these two sections of the island were united and Barbados took on its present shape. It became, in size, twenty-one miles long and fourteen miles wide, with an area of one hundred and sixty-six square miles. It rose, at its highest point, eleven hundred and four feet above the sea, and you may be glad to know that, since then, the upheavals which kept lifting the island out of the ocean have stopped completely.

One curious fact that you will notice is that there are old sea cliffs and terraces inside the island, one series surrounding the Christ Church ridge and another encircling the central upland (see map). Erdiston College

Old Sea Cliff with District 'C' Police Station in background

in St. Michael is built on a high cliff and District 'C' Police Station in St. Philip is built on another. The origin of all these cliffs and terraces is probably due to the way in which the island emerged from the sea. It must have risen by a number of jerking movements and at every pause the sea washed vigorously against its shores, cutting a cliff and a terrace, until after many, many years, with the island rising higher with each movement, the long flight of cliffs and terraces was completed as we now know it.

Further Reading

The Geology of Barbados
    by J. B. Harrison and A. J. Jukes-Browne.
The Uplift of Barbados by C. T. Trechmann.
The Antillean Caribbean Region by Charles Schuchert.
The Geography of the West Indies and Adjacent Lands
    by J. C. Cutteridge.

Chapter 5

THE MIRACLE OF CREATION

THE appearance of the island, when it emerged from the sea, was quite different from what it is at the present time. It was uncultivated and bare, and the rays of the tropical sun beat down unmercifully upon it. No human being could have lived in the conditions existing in the island at the time. There was no water to drink, no trees to give shade, no soil on which crops could be grown.

As the years rolled on, however, nature began to perform more of her miracles. The rain fell, the sun shone and the winds blew on the surface of the earth. The top of its rock formation was broken up and from the loose earth, which was thus produced, came the soil of Barbados. Gradually, the elements helped to produce the types of soil with which we are familiar to-day — the red and black soils of the coral area, the clay and white earth soil of the Scotland District.

If you go on the kind of expedition we have recommended, you will find that the Scotland District is completely different from the rest of the island. Four-fifths of the island's surface is covered with coral limestone which in some places is as thick as four hundred feet. But the Scotland District has no such coral capping and is composed of soft rocks, the surface of which is constantly being washed away by rain. The Scotland District is separated from the rest of the island by a far-reaching

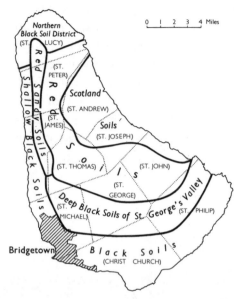

Sketch Map showing Kinds of Soil in Barbados

cliff which has been called the Great Limestone Cliff. You are probably familiar with Hackleton's Cliff in St. Joseph, but you should bear in mind that this is only a part of the Great Limestone Cliff.

At the beginning of its history as an island, Barbados must have been entirely covered with coral limestone. Then there came a time when the sea launched heavy onslaughts on the eastern coast and after a long while this broke up the coral cover on that part of the island. As a result, the soft rocks under the coral limestone became exposed and were rapidly worn away. That is how the area now called the Scotland District was formed.

The soft rocks of this area, measuring twenty-two square miles, are responsible for the problem of soil erosion we have to face to-day in certain parts of the island. The surface of the Scotland District is not covered with coral limestone like the rest of the island. There are springs at the base of the Great Limestone Cliff and from these sources of water little streams flow down towards the sea on the island's eastern shore. During the dry season there is no problem but, when the rain falls heavily, the streams become swollen torrents and they

Soil erosion and land slippage in the Scotland District. The Government is trying to check erosion here.

rapidly wear away the soft rocks on their way down to the ocean. At times, landslides occur, and roads, bridges and patches of cultivation slip away from their appointed places.

When Barbados came out of the ocean, the higher part of the island was tilted and thrust upwards towards the east and north, and it therefore received straight into its lap the north-east trade wind, which came all the way across the Atlantic from West Africa. As a result of this, the island's climate is quite cool and pleasant, although the mean temperature in Bridgetown during January is 76° and the temperature in August is 80°.

But the north-east trade wind, blowing strongly and steadily over the island, had one unfavourable result, as we shall now explain. When the rain fell, part of it soaked through the porous coral rock and went down to underground reservoirs. Some of it stayed on the surface to moisten the soil and to form ponds. But the trade winds tended to dry the soil quickly. This is why Barbados, in the years to come, was limited to growing certain crops. While Trinidad, St. Lucia and Dominica could grow a variety of crops, including fruit, Barbados, as you will see later, depended more and more on sugar because it was well suited to her soil and wind-swept condition.

The Ocean Current

The making of its soil was the first step in the preparation of the island as a suitable place for men to live in. Then the ocean currents began to play a part in the fascinating story. Barbados, which lies thirteen degrees north of the equator, is set in the path of the south equatorial current. This current flows from West Africa to South America, where a branch of it mingles with the Orinoco River and then flows into the Caribbean waters.

Fruit and seeds, which had remained fertile in spite of a long ocean journey, were brought by the south equatorial current from West Africa to the South American continent and from there to Trinidad and Barbados and other islands of the West Indies. On the coral beaches of Barbados to-day we can see many of the plants which were introduced to the island by the ocean current which had previously washed many distant and neighbouring lands before coming to us.

The south equatorial current was one of the wonder-workers that helped to create our island home. From the distant shores of West Africa, more than two thousand miles away, it brought the seeds and fruits that produce many of the plants which we can still see growing to-day — the sword bean, the gorse nicker, the burr grass and the wild lavender. From Guyana, Surinam and French Guiana came the sea-coconuts which, even at the present time, grow quite plentifully on our shores. From Trinidad and South America arrived the seeds of the plants that are now commonly seen on our beaches — the sea grape, the seaside lavender, the manchineel and the seaside spurge.

Seeds and fruit were not the only things transported to Barbados by this far-ranging ocean current. Debris and

Coconut Trees

driftwood were also conveyed to this island, sometimes bringing the germs of plants and sometimes animals of different kinds. It was in this way that the island received its first animals — the Barbados monkey and the racoon, several kinds of lizards and insects and a harmless type of snake. On one occasion in recent times, the ocean current presented us with an alligator from South America. Fortunately, this did not become a habit in primitive times or Barbados would not be as pleasant as it is to-day.

It is from the ocean current that we probably received some of the birds which are now regarded as native to the island. From the neighbouring lands probably came the blackbird, with its glossy coat and chirpy manner, the sparrow, greyish-brown in colour and the most intelligent of the Barbadian birds, the green-crested humming bird, the ground dove, small and grey, and apparently as fond of the earth as of the air, the pea-whittler, something like the sparrow, but easily recognised because of the shrill musical notes that gave it its name, and the rain-bird which pounced, like a hawk, on insects and lizards and did Barbados a great service by killing the destructive South American moths whenever they arrived in the island.

A Rain-Bird   A Ring-neck Plover

The Wind and the Birds

Next in importance to the ocean currents in the cultivation of the island were the winds which came to Barbados from the south-east during the rainy seasons. The northeast trade wind, coming as it does across the Atlantic Ocean, all the way from Africa, over two thousand miles away, can have played no part in the cultivation of Barbados. But it is quite probable that the southerly gales, which start in the northern part of South America, some two hundred and fifty miles away, brought certain substances that prepared the soil for higher plants, and then transported from the South American continent the living germs from which we obtained many of our plants.

The birds of the air also played their part in the miracle of transforming Barbados from a bare, arid land into a habitable place. Every year, as they do now, they escaped from the cold of North America and flew to the warmer regions of the southern continent. On their way down, they alighted on the lands of the Caribbean, bringing seeds in their crops or in the mud that stuck to their feet. They came then, as they come now, from the great northern regions, over two thousand miles away — the great blue heron, the sandy snipe, the blue gaulding, the Christmas bird and the belted kingfisher.

You can perhaps imagine these birds flying over such a long distance and pausing to feed at regular intervals on the lands they visited for a few hours. But can you imagine little birds like the pika and the plover, flying the whole distance without stopping at all and arriving at Barbados completely worn out? You will agree that such a feat of endurance could not be equalled by any human being, even if he had wings.

Thanks to the ocean current, the winds and the birds, plants began to grow and soon covered the stark nakedness of the island. The sea shores were shaded with beach trees and other parts of the island looked as if they had been cultivated by an unseen hand. For higher plants, some of which can still be seen to-day, were growing profusely in the interior.

If you get a chance to visit Turner's Hall Wood in the Scotland District or Foster Hall Wood beneath Hackleton's Cliff, you will see the kind of trees and vegetation that formed the ancient forests of Barbados many years ago. Those woods will give you some idea of how the island must have looked during the centuries when it lay sleeping in the sun, caressed by the trade wind, lapped by the waters of the ocean and waiting for the arrival of men who would clear away sites and build their settlements.

Further Reading

The Uplift of Barbados by C. T. Techmann.
Geology of Barbados by J. B. Harrison and A. J. Jakes-Browne.

Chapter 6

THE AMERINDIANS

THE Amerindians, with whom our ancestors are connected, came from the wide expanses of the Pacific Ocean and travelled across the vast areas of South America. Eventually they reached Brazil, Venezuela and the Guianas. From there they entered the Caribbean Sea and travelled from one territory of the West Indies to another.

Thanks to the investigations of Ronald Taylor and the late Professor R. P. Bullen, we now know that the first Amerindians to settle in Barbados were the Barrancoid people. The latter travelled from Venezuela to Trinidad and later to Barbados where they arrived at about the time of the birth of Christ.

The Barrancoid Indians left Barbados after a stay of some 600 years. They were followed 200 years later by the Arawaks who arrived here around A.D. 600. They were conquered by the Caribs who themselves disappeared from the island in A.D. 1500.

We know more about the Arawaks than of any of our Amerindian ancestors. When they came to Barbados they must have found the shape of the island much the same as it is at the present time. The southern part rose, as it does to-day, by a series of terraces, which were once coral reefs, to a ridge running east and west. This is now the Christ Church ridge, whose highest point is about six hundred feet above the sea.

North of this ridge was the low-lying land we now call the St. George's Valley, and from this the island rose again to a ridge in the centre which reached a height of just over one thousand feet above sea-level and embraced the present parishes of St. Joseph and St. Andrew.

The Arawaks must have been attracted to Barbados because it was well-wooded. Its gullies and valleys were thickly planted with tall trees and even the less fertile spots were covered with shrubs and vegetation of different sorts. From what we know of our native or indigenous trees we can imagine what the island looked like at that time.

The Indigenous Trees
The West Indian cedar, with its straight, smooth trunk, rose to a height of forty feet and its wood proved, in later years, to be of great value in making furniture. The fustic tree, with its oval and pointed leaves, spread its branches wide and offered a welcome shade. The Jack-in-a-box extended its branches from a tall, thick trunk and bore large, heart-shaped leaves. The lignum vitae, an evergreen tree, with long, stout branches, shed few of its leaves and flourished throughout the year. The locust tree grew fifty feet high with massive buttresses supporting its trunk at the base. Most of these trees can still be seen in various parts of the island.

There were also shade trees which grew in the open ground or in gullies where the soil was deep and fertile. These are as familiar to us as they must have been to the first Barbadians. To-day the silk cotton tree grows, as it grew many, many years ago, to a height of sixty feet, with roots that reach far up its trunk and seem to serve as buttresses. The Sand Box, a large, well-proportioned tree, with many branches, still flourishes to-day and its thick bark is covered as before, with short, sharp prickles. The cabbage palm raises its straight, slender trunk to a height of a hundred feet and the large leaves of its crown constantly sway in the breeze as they did in prehistoric times.

Perhaps the most important of these shade trees is the bearded fig. This tree still grows in the island as it must have done in the time of the Arawaks. It is a large upright tree with numerous branches from which sprout masses of roots which grow until they reach the ground. Can we

A Silk Cotton Tree in St. Philip's Church Yard

wonder that the bearded fig trees (los barbados) caught the fancy of the Portuguese and inspired them to give the island its name?

You now have some idea of the scene on which the Arawaks first gazed when they arrived in Barbados. They came to the West Indies from South America where their descendants still live to-day. They migrated northward, looking for new homes and settled in the Bahamas, the islands of the Greater Antilles and Trinidad.

Those who came to Barbados must have arrived in the island some time between A.D. 1000 and 1100. They found a land that was not as mountainous as some of the neighbouring islands. The rainfall was therefore lower than in other islands, though it was more than it is in Barbados to-day. The island had to thank its tall, massive trees for the great rainfall it enjoyed in those far-off days. The trees had a cooling effect on the air. They produced large quantities of water vapour which saturated the air and the surplus moisture was precipitated as rain.

The Arawak Settlement

The forests of Barbados were not large enough to provide good hunting, but the Arawaks did not depend on this for their living. They were interested in farming and were looking for a place where they could settle permanently. The island must have pleased them because its thin soil was suited for growing their crops. Except for its terraced uplands, the island was flat compared with other islands in the Caribbean and this, too, they must have considered good for their kind of agriculture.

The new arrivals did not take long to establish themselves in their island home. They built large settlements in the districts we now know as Pie Corner in St. Lucy, Silver Sands and Chancery Lane in Christ Church, and Indian River in St. Michael. All this we know to-day because learned men, whom we call archaeologists, have dug up and examined many of the tools, pottery, images and other relics that were left by these people. From their study of these relics they have been able to tell us a great deal about these early inhabitants of this island.

Water was one of the most serious problems facing the Arawaks. For this reason they settled not only on the coast but in districts where there were ponds and fresh water springs. It is believed, for instance, that they lived in villages in the neighbourhood of St. Andrew's Church, where there is a river, near St. Luke's Church in St. George, where there is a water-bearing gulley, and around Codrington College in St. John and Three Houses in St. Philip, where there are springs.

Pieces of Arawak Pottery in the Barbados Museum

Sometimes, too, they would pick out a river bed that led from the first of the terraced table lands right down to the sea and all along this they would set up their villages. They also established themselves in gulleys and caves that protected them against the storms and hurricanes that visited the island from time to time.

The main crops grown by the Arawaks were maize and cassava. Indeed, they were called 'Arawaks' because the word means 'cassava-eaters'. But, while they were fond of agriculture, which gave them their settled habits, their chief occupation was fishing. They avoided the windward coast because the sea there could be very rough, but they found that the coral reefs around the island supplied them with a great many fish. These they caught either with a net or a harpoon. They also used bows and arrows to catch fish as the Indians of other lands used to do.

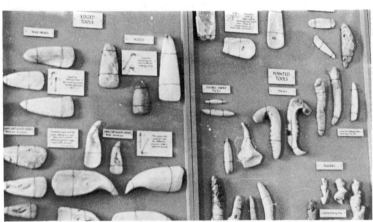

Arawak Shell Tools in the Barbados Museum

Their Social Life

Sometimes the Arawaks would go far out into the ocean on fishing expeditions and for this they used canoes or 'dugouts'. They made use of sheltered bays along the south and west coasts of the island to set up little 'ship building yards' where they made these canoes. They would get their material from the trees in the inland area and float them down the stream until they reached their 'shipyards'. It has been said that, just as every member of the modern Barbadian family helps in the stirring of the Christmas pudding or the decorating of the Christmas trees, so all the ancient Barbadians in the village, whether young or old, male or female, were expected to help in the building of these canoes.

The number of Arawaks who thus settled in Barbados probably ran to a total of several thousands. It is believed that the island was governed by a head-chief, who was advised by a council and had great power in times of peace and war. Under him were the headmen who ruled over the villages up and down the island.

The work of governing Barbados, in these prehistoric times, could not have been very difficult. For the Arawaks were a friendly, peaceful and law-abiding people. They were not cannibals, like the Caribs who roamed other parts of the West Indian region. Indeed, in some ways, they seemed to have reached quite a high standard of civilisation. For instance, they did not sacrifice human beings in their religion. Moreover, they practised mono-gamy — in other words, a man was allowed to have only one wife, though their leaders were not expected to follow this rule and could have several wives.

The Arawaks were a good-looking race of people. They were olive-skinned and of medium height. They had long, coarse, straight hair, broad shoulders and deep chests. The women, in particular, seemed proud of their black hair and wore it down to their hips. They had a peculiar custom of flattening the heads of their male infants by squeezing them with boards and this may be why the noses of the men were broader than those of the women. They wore little or no clothing and were fond of dancing and games. They lived in small round houses and slept in hammocks, a practice that was unknown to the people of Europe at that time.

Their Mysterious Disappearance

One of the strange things about the Amerindians — Barrancoids, Arawaks or Caribs — is that after living in Barbados for hundreds of years, with intervening periods between their settlements, they completely disappeared from the scene.

It may be that the ponds and springs of the island were dried up during a long period of drought and that the Amerindians were deprived of their sources of water. It may be that the Spaniards began to raid the island, looking for labourers to work in what is now known as Haiti and Hispaniola and forced the Caribs into slavery.

Whatever may have been the reason, it is known that that Caribs left the island around the year A.D. 1500.

After that Barbados was completely uninhabited for more than a hundred years. The island returned to its ancient state, growing wild with vegetation, and waiting for some one to arouse it again from its slumbers in the tropical sun.

Further Reading

The Pre-History of Barbados by G. Barton.
R. P. Bullen, *the B.M.H.S. Journal*, November 1966.
C. N. C. Roach, *the B.M.H.S. Journal*, Vol. VI, No. 2.

Chapter 7

THE STARVING TIME

THE Europeans who first came to Barbados were not English or Portuguese, but Spaniards. The latter came here shortly after Columbus discovered the New World in 1492 and found the Arawaks still living on the island. But when the Portuguese visited it in 1536, the Indians had already abandoned the island.

The Portuguese did not want to settle in Barbados and did not claim it for their country. But they thought it would be a good place to visit every now and again and they therefore let loose a number of wild hogs to make sure that, whenever they returned here, they would have a good supply of meat.

The first English ship to come to Barbados was the *Olive Blossom*. It arrived in 1625 with a number of colonists and the stores they needed to make a settlement. It was really going to another part of the Caribbean but, owing to the faulty seamanship of its sailing master, it was forced to make for Barbados.

These Englishmen found the island uninhabited, with woods growing right down to the water's edge. It looked so wild they thought it had never been settled before. They believed it looked like a fertile land and therefore took possession of it in the name of 'James, King of England'. They landed on the coast near what is now called Holetown in St. James and to-day you can see a monument there which was erected to their memory in 1905. One thing will interest you when you look closely at this monument and that is that the inscribed date of the *Olive Blossom's* arrival is wrong!

The visitors from the *Olive Blossom* did not stay long.

Holetown Monument

They merely rested for a while and then returned home. But when they reached England they gave so favourable a report of the island that their employer, Sir William Courteen, decided to send out a number of settlers. These arrived in Barbados on February 17th, 1627. They were eighty in number and brought with them ten Negroes whom they had captured from a prize on their way out.

They came provided with all the equipment to make a settlement and disembarked near the spot where the men of the *Olive Blossom* had landed two years before. They set about laying the foundation of a town which they called Jamestown, the early name of Holetown. They elected their own governor, John Powell, and courageously faced the future, knowing they would have to overcome many hardships before they could win a profitable living from the land.

One of the first difficulties that faced the settlers was that there were no roads. Whatever communications had been established by the Arawaks were now completely overgrown by trees and shrubs. Moreover, the land was frequently broken by gullies and this made the problem even more acute. The colonists brought in horses, mules and cattle to help them to get about. But they soon found that donkeys were better than horses on the rough tracks and that the most useful animals of all were the camels which they later imported from West Africa.

Their most pressing need was food to eat. They hunted the hogs the Portuguese had left, but these could not last them very long. Fortunately, the Governor of Essequibo, now a part of Guyana, came to their rescue, sending the Barbadians forty Arawaks along with a number of plants that would grow in the island. Thanks to the hard work of these Indians, the settlement soon began to flourish.

The plants then grown in Barbados are now familiar to all of us — yams, cassava, and Indian corn, plantains, bananas and oranges, lemons, pineapples and limes. From all this they got a good supply of food. In addition, they planted tobacco, cotton and indigo for export. Meanwhile, the settlement continued to grow, with more men, women and children arriving from England in a steady stream. By 1628 the population numbered nearly two thousand and all the able-bodied worked energetically, felling trees, building log houses, setting up forts and mounting them with guns.

But the prosperity of the new settlement did not last long. Soon the lean and hungry days of the first year returned and the settlers suffered even more miserably than before. Because of the difficulty of getting food, this period came to be known as the 'Starving Time'.

The new troubles of the island were largely caused by the dispute over its ownership. This led to several violent changes. One group of men would claim the island, but as soon as they tried to settle down they would be attacked by another group. For some time the settlers never really knew where they were. And all the while they went in fear of storms and hurricanes. They were always expecting to be attacked by the Spaniards or the Portuguese; and above all, there was the constant dread of starvation owing to the unsettled state of the island and the lack of rainfall.

The trouble of the settlers started this way. When the Earl of Carlisle heard how well Courteen's men were faring in Barbados, he began to bestir himself. Claiming that the island had previously been granted to him by the King, he sent out sixty-four settlers and appointed Charles Wolverstone as governor. These arrived in the middle of 1628 and settled in the area we now call Bridgetown. Wolverstone at once declared the Courteen settlers to be usurpers and summoned them to Bridgetown.

The Courteen men were bitterly disappointed when their second in command, William Dean, went over to the Carlisle men. But they continued to show their defiance under their governor, John Powell.

After a short period of peace, Powell did a dangerous thing. He captured Wolverstone and Dean and sent them in irons to England. This was the kind of game both sides could play. Before long, another Carlisle governor,

The Earl of Carlisle

Henry Hawley, arrived in Barbados. He enticed Powell on board his ship and sent him as a prisoner to England.

Hawley succeeded in establishing the Earl of Carlisle as the owner of Barbados. Then Sir William Tufton was appointed to succeed Hawley as governor of the island. He was an energetic man. He wanted to stop all the confusion and violence that had been troubling the settlement. He had a great deal of sympathy for the white indentured servants and tried to improve their lot. But he made himself powerful enemies and they set the Earl of Carlisle against him. Soon he was forced to give up his place as governor to Henry Hawley.

During all this time the island was going from bad to worse. The year 1630 was a period of severe drought. Like the Arawaks before them, the English settlers depended on ponds and springs for their water and when there was no rainfall for a long time the colony suffered a great deal. To help the settlers over this crisis the Earl of Carlisle sent out supplies until the island could grow its own food again. But the Barbadians suspected that Hawley was holding back most of these supplies and using them for himself and his friends. Tufton, who was still in the island, undertook to get up a memorial complaining about this. Henry Hawley was very annoyed. He summoned Tufton to appear before a special court where he was tried for high treason and later shot.

In spite of all these difficulties, the settlers held on grimly. And after a while things began to change and the 'Starving Time' became only an unhappy memory. Large crops of cotton and tobacco were produced and the island gained much profit from its export trade. This success was mainly due to the Dutch who helped the Barbadians by buying their tobacco and cotton and selling them clothing and provisions at lower prices than the English merchants. This was to bring trouble later on when England resolved to prevent free trade between her colonies and foreign nations. But for the time being the Barbadians felt that their efforts to establish the colony had brought them some reward.

Further Reading

A True and Exact History of the Island of Barbados
    by Richard Ligon.

Chapter 8

LAND AND FREEDOM

In the early days of the settlement, life in Barbados appealed only to the hardy pioneer. The houses were rude log cabins with low roofs. They were usually very hot because the settlers had the curious habit of building their windows on the leeward and not on the windward side. This they did to keep out the wind and the driving rain.

Trade was carried on by exchanging cotton and tobacco for the articles the Barbadians wanted from the traders and merchants who had already established themselves in their midst. Taxes were paid not in money but with quantities of the same crops.

The settlers kept to the west coast of the island because of the great difficulty of getting from one place to another. When they tried to extend their fields, the monkeys and racoons came out of the woods and attacked their crops, while rats invaded their houses in large numbers. Moreover, they were troubled with such pests as mosquitoes and flies, cockroaches and ants.

But gradually conditions began to improve. More and more settlers came out to Barbados. By 1638, there were 6,000 white colonists in the island and by 1643 this number had risen to more than 37,000.

Up and down the island, there was strenuous activity. A rough and ready road was built from Scotland District to Speightstown and routes were cleared, linking a number of plantations with Consett Bay in St. John and the Crane in St. Philip. Highways were constructed connecting Bridgetown and Speightstown and well-built stone houses began to make their appearance in both of these towns.

Indentured Servants

Barbados fared well at this stage because it attracted settlers who were looking for land and a chance to establish their fortunes as independent yeomen. This was the secret of the island's success in the early days. The first settlers came out to the island largely because they were given small plots of five or ten acres on which they could settle as self-respecting landowners.

Then other efforts were made to attract more settlers. If a man was too poor to travel from England to Barbados at his own expense, he could be brought out as an indentured servant. He would sign an agreement to work for a planter for five or seven years and in return his master would pay his passage out, feed, clothe and shelter him in the island, and at the end of his term of service he would give him a small plot of land or a small sum of money with which he could buy the land. It was by this method that the island began to get a large number of men, women and children to build up the settlement.

There were times, however, when the indentured servants did not receive anything like the treatment they expected in the island. Some of them were lucky to serve good masters and were treated kindly. But others suffered a great deal from neglect and cruelty. They were made to work in the field from six in the morning till six in the evening, with a two-hour break in the middle of the day. Those who did not labour in the open fields, under the scorching sun, were set to work, after the introduction of sugar, in the mills or the boiling rooms where the furnaces at times made their task unbearable for men accustomed to a cold climate.

All they were given to eat was cold lobolly — now known to all of us as 'koo-koo' — and potato roots. They slept at night on bare boards with nothing to cover them. If they complained, they were flogged at the whipping posts. If they resisted, they were treated like the beasts of the field. You will not be surprised to learn that in 1649 these white servants rose up in revolt against their pitiful lot. They planned to kill all their employers and make themselves masters of the island. But the rebellion was nipped in the bud and the ringleaders were punished unmercifully.

Indeed, it is believed that the white servants were treated, in some respects, even worse than the African slaves of whom you will read in the next chapter. The masters knew that their term of service was limited to a few years and therefore tried to get all the work they could out of them before they won their freedom. But the white servants had at least one advantage over the African slaves — if they lived long enough, they would become free men and own a small plot of land. This was the great thing that kept attracting men and women to Barbados and sustained them in all their suffering. They knew that, as landowners, they would become members of a free community and for this reason they were prepared to run great risks.

An Independent Spirit

The spirit that governed Barbados in those days was a sturdy and independent one. The settlers cultivated the land in time of peace and were ever ready to defend the country in time of war. They were a proud and spirited people. They claimed they were entitled to the same rights as Englishmen living in England and that they would prefer to die rather than give up those rights.

At the outset the Earl of Carlisle had promised them certain privileges but that promise was not fulfilled at the time. Therefore, when Henry Hawley, of whom I wrote in the previous chapter, called the first Parliament of Barbados, he was eagerly supported by the Barbadians. Up to that time, Hawley had been very unpopular. His execution of Sir William Tufton was regarded as unjust. Moreover, as Governor of Barbados, he had done many things to annoy the settlers. But, when he came forth as the champion of self-government, he was hailed on all sides with enthusiasm.

That was in 1639 — a date you should remember because the House of Assembly was started then. If you are a stamp-collector, you may have seen the special stamp which was issued in 1939 to commemorate the three hundredth anniversary of the House of Assembly.

When Oliver Cromwell became master of England, Barbados refused to acknowledge the victory of the English Parliament and Sir George Ayscue was sent out with a squadron of ships to reduce the island to submission. On this occasion, the Barbadians were moved by the same spirit of independence and it took Ayscue two months before he could establish himself in the island. Even then he could not get its submission until he guaranteed that Barbados would not lose her freedom. This was done by the Articles of Agreement which were signed at the Mermaid Tavern in Oistin in 1652 and are sometimes referred to as the Magna Carta of Barbados.

These Articles laid it down that the Government of Barbados should consist of a Governor, appointed from England, a Council, which was to be appointed by him, and an Assembly, which was to be elected by the settlers. In a later chapter you will see that this, in spite of all the changes that have taken place during the past three hundred years, is still substantially our system of government to-day. In addition, the Articles made it clear that the rights of the Barbadians should be equal to those

Sir George Ayscue

enjoyed by Englishmen at home and that no taxes should be imposed on them without the consent of their elected representatives. This was a great victory and could only have been won by a community where the land was divided into freeholds and held by yeoman farmers who believed they were as independent as anyone else in the world.

Here we see Barbados as a European society in the early days. The settlers had come mostly from the British Isles, but their origins were of different kinds. Some were members of the best English families, while others were political prisoners of some importance who were deported for whatever mistakes they had committed. The rest were simple peasant folk who had come to Barbados either by force or of their own free will in the hope that they would find the island a land of opportunity. But the vital thing was that every free man had a stake of some sort in the country and they were proud of the system of parliamentary government they had won from the Mother Country.

Further Reading

The History of Barbados by John Poyer.

Chapter 9

SUGAR AND SLAVERY

BARBADOS did not continue as a free country for a long time. The vigour of the Island was largely due to the spirit of the yeoman farmers who owned much of the land. Its prosperity was due to the variety of small crops it produced. But the main crop of the island was tobacco and this soon ran into difficulties. First, Barbadian tobacco, when imported into England, had to bear heavier duties than American tobacco. Then the American Colonies took to producing more and more tobacco, with the result that its price began to fall and the Barbadians could not make the same profits as before.

It was when they were faced with this threat to their prosperity that the Barbadians learnt about the great success with which the Dutch were producing sugar in Brazil. They heard that three times as much sugar as

Old Windmill at Kirtons, St. Philip

tobacco could be produced

from a given piece of land and they hurried to South America to learn the best methods from the Dutch. To grind the sugar cane, mills were introduced, driven first by horses and then by cattle. Later windmills were set up as being better still, and the island became a hive of activity. At Lowland plantation in Christ Church and at Kirtons in St. Philip you can still see the sort of windmill which was used to grind sugar cane many years ago.

From Small Holdings to Plantations

Barbados now began to concentrate more and more on sugar and a number of important things happened. The island had to import most of its food and there was great anxiety when supplies did not arrive in time. The yeoman farmers, who grew small crops, were unable to make money from the new industry. Sugar called for large plantations and the small farmers did not have the money to buy sufficient land or to set up sugar works. More and more land passed into the hands of a few wealthy men and the small-holders were gradually squeezed out of business.

As the sugar industry developed, the planters looked about for the cheapest means of production. They discovered that African slaves could work much harder in a tropical climate than white indentured servants. They learnt that it took just as much money to purchase a white man's labour for ten years as to buy an African slave for life. No wonder the planters set about importing Negroes in large numbers.

By 1643, when the sugar industry was already establishing itself, there were nearly 6,000 Negroes in the
island. Some twenty years later, the number of slaves had
risen to about 50,000, and at the same time the white
population had declined to 25,000. This trend was to
become even more marked as sugar assumed greater
importance in the island's economy.

The white small farmers, seeing that they had no hope
of making a good livelihood in Barbados, began to emigrate
in large numbers, going to such places as Surinam and
Jamaica, Guadeloupe, Martinique and Marie Galante,
Grenada, Tobago and Curacao, Virginia and New
England. With thousands of small farmers going abroad
and thousands of African slaves coming in, the pattern
of Barbadian society as we know it to-day was soon to
be set.

Attempts were still made from time to time to keep
the island supplied with white settlers. No one would
now come out willingly, as before, because there were
no prospects of owning land. But Oliver Cromwell started
the idea of sending people out by force and this went on
for a long time. Cavaliers were sent out from England
during the civil war. Men were sent out from Ireland in
1649 after the Irish Rebellion and from England after the
Monmouth Rebellion in 1685. Sometimes they were given
the choice of doing field work in Barbados or serving a
term of imprisonment in the Tower of London.

For these men there was little hope now that Barbados
had changed from a peasant to a plantation economy.

Those who could escaped. Many who survived their service in the island emigrated to other countries. Some moved to Bridgetown and made their way in commerce, while others seized what little opportunity there was in agriculture and in due course established themselves as members of the island's planter society. But many were left to drag out a wretched life in the depressed areas of Barbados. Even to-day we can see the descendants of these men, now called 'poor whites', living in districts like Newcastle in St. John and in certain parts of Scotland District.

African Slaves

The Negro slaves came to Barbados and other territories of the West Indies from the Grain Coast, the Ivory Coast and the Slave Coast of West Africa. They were imported from that extensive part of the African continent which includes the modern states of Guinea and Sierra Leone, Liberia and the Ivory Coast, Ghana and Togo, Dahomey, Nigeria and the Cameroons. They came, speaking a variety of languages, from groups whose way of life was based on different customs and different cultural patterns. There were the Eboes, gentle and timid souls, who at times were driven to suicide to escape their melancholy fate. There were the Pawpaws who applied themselves, with almost incredible cheerfulness, to their labours in a new world. And there were the fierce and warlike Koromantyns who reacted against harsh treatment with a bitter and implacable resentment.

The ships that transported them also brought bees-wax from which the Barbadians made candles to use as lights when the candles from England failed them. From West Africa, too, came the wool-less sheep, which supplied the island with mutton, the African monkeys, whose descendants can still be seen to-day, and the camels which were used as transport when the colonists travelled long distances over rough roads. The slave ships also introduced Barbados to Guinea corn, which proved a popular dish from then up to the present time.

But the slave ships brought other things that were less pleasant. So filthy were the vessels and so crowded were the slaves that germs and diseases invaded the island in large numbers. Yellow fever was one of these diseases and so dreadful was it that it killed 6,000 people in 1647. The dead were so numerous that they could not be buried properly and were dumped in a swamp just outside Bridgetown. It is no wonder that Barbados began to lose the good name it had as a healthy island.

The life of the Negro slaves was grim indeed. They arrived on the slave ships stark naked, after crossing the dreaded 'Middle Passage' from West Africa to the Caribbean. They were sold to the planters and were immediately marched off to the plantations where they were to spend a life of toil and sweat. Each man was given a wife as a companion and, if he proved a good worker, he was rewarded with two or three wives.

The slaves lived in small huts of wattle and thatch and slept on boards like the white servants. When a horse died on the plantation, there was much rejoicing for they knew they would get it all to eat. When an ox was killed, they had no share in the feast that followed. But, if such an animal died, the slaves rejoiced even if it died of disease because they knew they would get the head, the skin and the intestines. The white servants had the doubtful pleasure of eating the body of the dead animal.

When a slave was ill, he would sometimes be given a little rum or kill-devil, as it was called, to cheer him up. Like the white servant, he worked from Monday to Saturday, from six o'clock in the morning to six in the evening, with a break for his midday meal from 11 a.m. to 1 p.m. After work was supper, and after supper, bed.

Sunday was a day of rest, though some of the slaves spent most of the day working for themselves. But most of them managed to get a little recreation. They were fond of music and dancing and would use kettledrums to provide a sort of orchestra. At times they also took to wrestling. Like some Barbadians to-day, the wrestlers were good at butting opponents with their heads and whoever was best at this would win the wrestling bout.

A Changed Society

Though the slaves could snatch a little enjoyment on their day of rest, you must not imagine that they were happy in their captivity. Most of them came from spirited African tribes and bitterly resented the loss of their freedom. Fortunately for the planters, the slaves could generally be kept from planning an island-wide revolt because they came from different tribes and spoke different languages.

In spite of this, the slaves in 1675 conspired to rise up and kill every white person in the island. But the plot was discovered before it could be carried out. So alarmed were the planters that they punished the ringleaders without mercy. Some of them were beheaded as a warning to others. Some were burnt alive and their bodies dragged through the streets to strike terror in the rebels' hearts.

All of this shows you what a great change came over the island after it gave up tobacco and other small crops and went in for sugar on a large scale. The small holdings were swallowed up by the large plantations. The yeoman farmer was pushed out by the big planter. The place of the white indentured servant was taken by the African slave. Barbados ceased to be a white community and became an island with a large Negro majority. It was no longer a free country, with small farmers cultivating their own plots of land and ready to defend the island in time of war. It became, instead, an unsettled land, with a minority of white planters and overseers nervously trying to hold down a large population of African slaves.

Further Reading

A History of Barbados 1625-1685 by Vincent T. Harlow.
Cavaliers and Roundheads in Barbados by D. Davis.
A Short History of the West Indies
    by J. H. Parry and P. M. Sherlock.

Chapter 10

THE CAPITAL AND CHIEF PORT

YOU have already learnt that, when the first English colonists came to Barbados, they built a settlement in Jamestown, which is now known as Holetown in the parish of St. James. Later, the Earl of Carlisle sent his own settlers and they set themselves up in what is now the city of Bridgetown in the parish of St. Michael.

As the colony of Barbados grew and prospered, settlers had to decide where to establish their capital and chief

An Early Map of Barbados

port. Bridgetown was being rapidly developed as a centre of trade. But Holetown (the Hole) was also getting its share of business and Oistins in Christ Church was quite a flourishing little village.

Speightstown, then and now the second largest town in the island, was setting itself up in the parish of St. Peter as the shipping centre for the north and east of Barbados. Soon it was to be called little Bristol because of the trade it carried on with the English town of Bristol.

Our ancestors had to consider a number of points very carefully before they decided on their capital and principal port. They had to choose a place which was on the leeward side of the island, sheltered from the trade winds that blow constantly from the East and North-East. This seemed to rule out Oistins.

They wanted a port that provided a natural harbour, with a safe anchorage for ships. This ruled out Holetown which was quite inadequate for the purpose. The choice now lay, therefore, between Speightstown and Bridgetown, with their natural indentations. If you examine these two towns, you will agree that our ancestors were right in selecting Bridgetown as their capital.

A Thriving Centre
In the early days, Bridgetown was not a healthy place to live in. There was a large swamp nearby, constantly fed by a sluggish stream, which often made the inhabitants of the town very ill. Yet the settlers realised it was the best spot in the island for landing and shipping goods and

they worked very hard to make it into a thriving centre.

They built houses, first of timber, then of stone. They constructed store-houses and places of business where planters and merchants met to exchange their goods. The planters disposed of their articles, sugar and tobacco, cotton and indigo, while they bought from the merchants the many necessities which were imported from abroad.

In the days before good roads were built, camels and donkeys were a familiar sight in Bridgetown. They brought the produce of the plantations to the town and, on the return trip to the country, their backs were laden with the many stores needed for the estates and with the household goods required by the planters' families.

Camels are no longer seen in the island to-day but at that time they must have been extremely useful. Any one of them, if he was a good specimen, could carry produce and stores that weighed as much as 1,600 pounds.

Though Bridgetown was an unhealthy place, where men and women had to work very hard, its inhabitants seemed to find time to relax and enjoy themselves. There were taverns where people could eat, drink and be merry after a day of strenuous labour. Some of these were highly respectable places where the planters could be frequently seen enjoying a feast. Indeed, one of them, kept by Master John Jobson, became very famous because it was the meeting-place of the island's Parliament.

Those who wanted less fashionable resorts could go to more humble places. There were quite a number of shops to which people went when they wanted to refresh themselves with a drink of rum, the popular by-product of the island's main industry.

The early settlers were not afraid to admit their weaknesses and referred to these places quite frankly as 'grog-shops'. Life was hard and uncertain and it is not surprising that the inhabitants frequently sought a stimulant to relieve themselves of their cares.

A Wise Decision

A number of geographical factors made Bridgetown the best site for the island's capital and chief port. It was situated at the end of a dry gully and the inner harbour provided excellent anchorage for schooners with a draught of less than twenty feet. Moreover, it served as a natural focus for all the fertile areas of the island since it was situated at a point of the coast approximately in the middle of the Limestone Lands and within equal reach from the most distant parts of the north or east of the country. The owner of a sugar factory in the most northerly parish, St. Lucy, or in the extreme east, St. Philip, would have about the same distance to travel in transporting his canes to Bridgetown.

Furthermore, the early settlers saw the great advantage that Barbados would enjoy as the most easterly of the West Indian Islands. They knew that its geographical position, with Carlisle Bay, an open roadstead leading straight into the Atlantic, would be favourable to trade and bring a steadily increasing revenue in the future.

Almost from the outset, Bridgetown proved its unique

value as the first port of call for any ship coming from Europe to the West Indies. It was natural for such ships to come to Barbados first because the tides and currents helped them on their way. In this way, Bridgetown became a great transhipment centre. For the cargo which was later sent on to the smaller islands was landed in the port before the ships sailed on to the larger islands.

Indeed, the tides and currents made it easy for ships to sail to this island from England, from Ireland and from South America. Thus it was that several important things happened. More and more settlers kept coming out from the Mother Country, because it was comparatively easy to get here, and they managed to keep in constant touch with their fellow countrymen at home. Barbados became the first port of call for the slave ships that brought their human cargo from Africa and before long Barbados became the West Indian centre for ships travelling from Europe to North and South America.

On Board a Slave Ship

In the early days of its history, as at the present time, the prosperity of the island depended largely on the size of the sugar crop and the prices it obtained for sugar and its by-products, molasses and rum. At first the sugar crop was transported to Bridgetown with considerable difficulty. Plantations which were on the windward side of the island had to ship their crop at Consett Bay in St. John and the Crane in St. Philip and from there it was brought by sea to Bridgetown.

Gradually this method of transportation, as well as that by camels and donkeys, was abandoned as good roads were constructed, linking the remoter parts of the island with the capital. The building of such roads was not very difficult because the island was comparatively flat, the gently sloping terraces or old seacliffs behind the town making communications between Bridgetown and the rest of the island a relatively easy matter. Within a comparatively short time, as many as one hundred ships a year called at Carlisle Bay, bringing what the island needed and taking away the products. And, as the years went by, Bridgetown grew in importance and the wise decision of the early settlers to make it the capital and chief port of the island was abundantly justified.

Further Reading

Historic Bridgetown by Warren Alleyne.

Chapter 11

THE ISLAND GARRISON

THE pattern of Barbadian life was now set for many years to come. There was not enough rainfall to enable the island to produce rice, as Guyana does to-day. Our soil was not sufficiently fertile to produce cocoa like Trinidad or bananas in large quantities like Jamaica. Since most of the island was wind-swept, it could not produce the same variety of crops as other West Indian islands, such as citrus fruits—oranges and tangerines, grapefruit and limes—and coconuts.

Sugar cane was the sort of crop that would grow in any tropical island and it was ideally suited to Barbados for several reasons. In the early days, the trade wind drove the windmills and the comparative flatness of the island made it easy to transport the crop to the various centres. The climate, with the abundant sunshine, was just right for the sugar content of the cane. The soil, with its natural drainage, was the kind in which sugar could be cultivated intensely.

We have already told you why tobacco was abandoned by the island as its staple crop. The other main crop left was cotton, but this, like cacao, bananas and citrus fruits, suffered from the effects of strong winds and needed protection by windbreaks of Guinea corn and similar crops. But sugar could grow both in the wind-swept highlands and in the moister flat lands.

The Plantocracy

It is small wonder that Barbados was the first island in the British Caribbean to grow sugar. With its large labour force, it now set out to become one of the most important sugar lands in the British Empire. The new pattern of Barbadian economy may be explained in one sentence. It became an island which produced sugar in large quantities and depended on the outside world almost entirely for its foodstuffs.

The planters, who ran the sugar industry, were now really in control of Barbados. They were resolved to take the fullest advantage of the island's geography. They set out to make as much money as they could in the shortest possible time.

They hardened their hearts to the sufferings of the 'poor whites' and the evils of African slavery. Though they could not allow the men and women under them to have any freedom, they demanded that they themselves should enjoy all the rights and privileges of Englishmen living at home.

Yet the planters had certain qualities that made them an interesting set of people. They were men of courage and enterprise, not easily daunted when things went wrong. Sometimes they were set back by periods of severe drought. They were worried by pests and plant diseases. They were harassed by cane fires which were set alight by the slaves to show their discontent. And they were ever faced with the danger of a large-scale slave revolt.

In addition, for a long period — from 1663 to 1837 — they were burdened with an export duty of 4½ per cent on all their produce. This really meant that they had to pay England about 10 per cent of all the profits they made in the island. But all these dangers and difficulties were met with the kind of spirit and resources that are found only in pioneers.

There was one thing that was especially remarkable about these men. They were not like the absentee proprietors of the eighteenth century whose only aim was to make all the money they could out of Barbados and live in England. The planters, in spite of all the difficult situations that faced them at times, were determined to make Barbados their home. With all their faults, they were Barbadians at heart. They intended not only that they themselves should live in the island but that their descendants should do the same thing for many years to come. This can be seen from the kind of houses they built — solid structures, some of which have survived right down to the present time.

Historic Buildings

Let us take a look at the houses that were built more than three hundred years ago. Holborn in Fontabelle, St. Michael, was probably the first of its kind to be built in Barbados. Unfortunately it was heavily damaged by the hurricane of 1831 and, when the house was rebuilt, its seventeenth century architecture was not completely restored.

Holborn House

But it was still a landmark in our history. It had once been the residence of the Governor of Barbados and still looked like an important mansion. It was a two-storeyed building with verandahs looking like arcades and with a long driveway lined with Royal Palms; anyone who got past the walls and the iron gate would find this path menaced by two sentry houses that stood guard on either side of the entrance. It was possible to see from this ancient mansion that, while the planters of the seventeenth century decided to make Barbados their home, they were quite prepared to protect themselves from any danger.

It was decided a few years ago to demolish Holborn in order to make way for commercial expansion in the area around the new harbour. To some, this was a source of considerable regret. But there was no widespread opposition to its demolition owing to the fact that Holborn had lost much of its original character.

There are two other houses, Nicholas Abbey in St. Peter and Drax Hall in St. George, which have survived the three worst hurricanes in Barbadian History.

Perhaps we should mention here that Barbados lies almost out of the track of hurricanes. But, now and again, it has been struck by fearful storms, as in 1675, 1780 and 1831. In 1955 we were visited by a hurricane that killed thirty-five persons and did heavy damage to houses, fruit trees and food crops. But this hurricane was in no

Nicholas Abbey

way comparable to the three great storms referred to above.

Both Nicholas Abbey and Drax Hall were built in the style of architecture which was popular among the gentlemen of England who could afford to build manor houses in the seventeenth century. Their one difference was that they were built of coral stone, but they have the same gable roofs running lengthwise as their English models, with other gables on the side to let in light and air.

Drax Hall, which was built by James Drax, the man whose genius was mainly responsible for the success of the sugar industry in Barbados, is particularly interesting because of its staircase. It is said to be the only example in the New World of the kind of stairbuilding that was adopted in England during the reign of James I. At the foot of the staircase is a broad arch made of woodwork in the style of the seventeenth century. It is believed that the walls of the rooms were also covered with woodwork that was done by some of England's most skilful craftsmen more than three hundred years ago, but this has been destroyed by the passing of time.

A visit to these two houses is well worth your while not only because of their association with the history of Barbados but because of their style of architecture. We should take pride in them because, as Mr. Thomas T. Waterman has written, they are the finest British colonial houses to be found anywhere in the New World. Indeed, they help to give us the impression that in Barbados, perhaps more than in any other West Indian island, there is a long tradition of stable government and civilised living.

A Hazardous Position

Though the planters faced the future with courage, they could not close their eyes to the hazards of a society based on slave labour. Their position was such that they were careful to make sure that an uprising of the slaves never took them by surprise. In the earliest days, before signal stations were set up, if anyone heard of any trouble he would at once discharge his musket and his neighbour would take up the alarm and pass it on until the whole island had been aroused by a long series of musket shots.

What gave the planters their best hope of security was the presence of armed forces in the island. There was a strong militia in which all free men were required to serve for a period and steps were taken from time to time to attract white immigrants who could help in the defence of the island. By the beginning of the eighteenth century Barbados had 22 forts and a number of batteries with a total of more than 460 guns.

Since it was the most eastern island of the Caribbean, it was regarded by the Mother Country as an important strategic outpost. To defend it first against the Dutch and in later years against the French, it was made an island garrison, with trenches, ramparts and forts along the sea coast. Charles Fort in St. Michael, with its 40 guns, was a formidable defence and there were strong batteries at such places as Holetown, Reid's Bay and

Speightstown. More and more forts were built until the citadel of St. Anne's Fort was constructed around 1705 in honour of Queen Anne.

In due course, the island's fortifications and batteries were taken over by the British Government and Barbados became the headquarters of the British troops in the Windward and Leeward Islands. The Lieutenant-General, who commanded all these troops, lived in Barbados. The Queen's Park we know to-day was his private residence and the present recreation centre and playing field formed the spacious grounds where he entertained his friends.

The Social Whirl

The soldiers stationed in Barbados lived in St. Anne's Fort and the military barracks surrounding the Garrison Savannah. This was the centre of social life in the island. Every evening the ladies and gentlemen who lived in and around the military establishment of St. Anne's, would drive out to Hastings and Worthing to enjoy the cool sea breezes. Then they would return to the Savannah — regarded at the time as the finest parade ground in the West Indies — where the regimental bands would entertain them with delightful music.

By calling imagination to our aid, we can easily visualise the social whirl of those days, the horses and carriages of the aristocracy, the young bloods and their ladies flaunting their skill on horseback, the handsomely dressed soldiers basking in the admiration of young and old alike. It was a time of gay and gracious living for those who moved in the island's best society. And this elegant life was enjoyed not only by the military but by the planters, merchants and professional men of the island.

St. Anne's Fort was linked with a number of signal stations whose messages could cover the whole island. It was connected by signal with Charles Fort nearby on the coast, with the Lieutenant-General's residence in Queen's Park, with Highgate, which commanded a view of the Harbour, with Gun Hill in St. George, which commanded an even wider view, with Moncrieffe in St. John and Cotton Tower in St. Joseph.

The signals which went from station to station summoned members to meetings of the Executive Council

Parade on the Garrison Savannah

and gave news of the arrival of ships. But the stations also looked after the grim business of warning the island that it was about to be attacked from the sea or that slaves were planning a revolt.

Thus behind the gaiety of the social scene there was always the reminder that the foundations of the island's prosperity were shaky since they were based on the labour of spirited and discontented African slaves.

Further Reading

The History of Barbados by R. Schomburgk.
Journals of the Barbados Museum and Historical Society.

Chapter 12

THE PLANTATION SYSTEM

THE sugar plantation in Barbados was the centre and core of the island's existence during the eighteenth century. The success of the plantation depended on the quality of its management, the efficiency of its labour force and the amount of money that was invested in it. The whole prosperity of the island rested on this system and it is worth our while to investigate how it worked and what kind of people it employed. But before we do this, we should have a look at the general situation in Barbados during this period.

The eighteenth century was a time of ups and downs for the island. Whenever England went to war with another country, this brought special worries for the Barbadians because they did not know where they would get their supplies from and what would become of their markets. At times during the century the sugar industry enjoyed a boom of prosperity and at others it seemed to hover on the brink of bankruptcy. In 1731 the island was visited by a disastrous hurricane and some fifty years later it was almost entirely destroyed by an even more calamitous one.

Barbados used to carry on a prosperous trade with the American Colonies but this was stopped after the American Revolution in 1775. This was a great blow to the islanders because they used to export sugar, rum, molasses

and other products to New England in return for supplies
of such essential things as beef, meal, fish and lumber. It
is true that the Barbadians then resorted to smuggling,
but they never fully recovered from the loss of the
American market. Thus when the American Colonies
won their independence, Barbados lost a large measure
of her prosperity.

Spacious Living

The small planter, who had been an important figure in
the island during its early years, could never have coped
with the crises that threatened the sugar industry from
time to time in the eighteenth century. Such a situation
could have been met only by the big planters who had
taken the place of the yeoman farmers. These men
succeeded where the yeoman farmers would have failed
because they had much more money and could therefore
stand the losses that every crisis brought upon them.
They were undoubtedly men with a spirit of adventure
and were prepared to take big risks in the hope of win-
ning great profits. And what made their efforts worthwhile
was that, in spite of all the difficulties that beset the sugar
industry, prices remained at a fairly high level for a long
time.

The planters of this period were not such thorough-
going Barbadians as their predecessors of the seventeenth
century. Some of them lived in England, regarding Barbados merely as a large plantation from which they made
their money. They were men of great wealth and enjoyed

a considerable influence among the ruling class of England. But those who lived in Barbados did much to establish a high standard of civilised living. Their tables were served with the finest dishes and many of them imported French brandy to make their punches, leaving rum to their less fortunate contemporaries. They entertained their friends by taking them on tours round the island in their pleasure boats. They moved around in carriages with large numbers of liveried attendants like the English aristocracy. Certainly their style of living was as magnificent as that of the English nobility of the time. And they were inferior to no other patrician class in the practice of a generous hospitality and in the art of spacious living.

The Manager

The wealth of the planter aristocrat came from the output of the sugar plantation. The all-absorbing task of those employed on the plantation was to raise a crop of sugar and prepare it for market. The management of an estate was a difficult and complicated business. Large sums of money were required to buy the expensive machinery and equipment that were necessary to manufacture sugar, molasses and rum. That was one of the main items that called for heavy investment by the planters.

In addition to this machinery and equipment, no plantation was complete without horses and donkeys and cattle. Such animals were necessary not only because they helped in the business of production but because, according to the agricultural practice of the time, their manure was essential for fertilising the soil. To keep a plantation well stocked with cattle was one of the main responsibilities of those who were entrusted with the burden of management.

The manager was perhaps the most important single person on the plantation. He was charged with arduous and exacting duties which began when the sugar crop was planted and never ended until the finished product arrived at its market. He had to see that the buildings and equipment of the plantation were kept in good condition. If the owner of the estate lived abroad, the manager had to keep in close touch with the 'attorney' who was the representative of the owner. He employed agents to look after the shipping of the sugar, rum and molasses after they were conveyed to Bridgetown and it was his responsibility to make sure that these agents were thoroughly reliable men.

Above all, it was the manager's duty to see that the plantation was always supplied with slaves in adequate numbers. Any time that the labour force fell below a certain point, the working of the plantation was certain to become inefficient. The manager was required to cope with all these problems and, no matter how difficult or complex they might be, he was expected to show a profit at the end of the year.

The Labour Force
When all is said and done, however, there was no factor

in the work of sugar production which was more important than the labour of the African slaves. The success of the plantation depended on whether it had a sufficient number of trained slaves to attend to its many activities. It was of the first importance to have slaves who were experienced workers. If they were 'green', a great deal of time had to be spent training them and, what is more, the new slaves tended to upset the older ones because they were very rebellious until they were broken in. A manager considered himself very lucky if he had a stable labour force.

Many slaves were needed to work a plantation efficiently. It took about fifty slaves a day to dig the necessary number of cane-holes in an acre of land. This work

Slaves Cane-holeing

was done with hoes and then the slaves planted the canes. Then followed the task of weeding and fertilising the ground and, when the crop was ready, the slaves cut the canes with 'bills' in the same way as they cut them to-day. It was hard labour, calling for a certain degree of skill and, if a plantation did not have experienced workers, a great deal of damage could be done.

The slaves who worked in the mills did not have to work as hard as the field slaves. Yet here even more skill was required and a plantation was greatly handicapped if time had to be spent training inexperienced slaves for these special tasks.

You will now understand why a plantation was regarded as such a vast undertaking. The problems which arose in the manufacture of sugar and its by-products were many

Slaves Working in a Sugar Mill, 1849

and varied. No one could foretell the exact size of the crop from year to year. No one could predict what the weather would be like — if the rain would be adequate, if the wind would be favourable, if a hurricane would destroy the work of all those employed on a plantation. The only thing one could be sure of was that nothing was really certain. Yet the work on the plantation always went on and, in spite of everything, the sugar industry, though not as prosperous as in the early days, brought the island a great deal of wealth.

Further Reading

Codrington Chronicle edited by Frank J. Klingberg.
Making of the West Indies
    by F. R. Angier, S. C. Gordon, D. G. Hall and M. Rekord.

Chapter 13

EMANCIPATION

FOR many years after African slaves were brought to
Barbados, no one was allowed to make them Christians.
In the French and Spanish Colonies, it was quite different.
There it was insisted that the slaves should be converted
to Christianity. But in Barbados and all the other British
colonies no one seemed to think that the slave possessed
an immortal soul and that he should be admitted to the
sacraments of the Christian religion.

The reason for this was that to instruct the slaves in
the Christian religion you first had to teach them English.
This was considered dangerous to the peace of the island
because, when the slaves came to Barbados, they spoke
different dialects and therefore could not get together
easily to organise revolts; whereas, if they were now
taught one common language, they would be able to
understand each other and could plan an uprising more
easily against their masters.

But there was one Barbadian who did not agree with
the planters of the British West Indies. His name was
Christopher Codrington and we have to give him a
special place in Barbadian history because his views were
unique for a planter aristocrat of the eighteenth century.
He believed that the slave was a human being and that
he should be treated kindly even when he rose up in
revolt. And at his death Codrington left two plantations

Statue of
Christopher Codrington

in Barbados, Society and
Consett, the profits of which
were to be used to educate
and Christianise the African
slaves.

The Codrington Experiment

The running of the plant-
ations along the lines recommended by Codrington was
by no means easy. For one
thing, the policy followed in
the Codrington estates was
viewed with suspicion and
alarm in an island which
felt, quite rightly, that such
a policy would undermine the whole foundation of
slavery. Still, the work went slowly and painfully on.
The slaves were baptized and instructed. They were
taught to read and write and Codrington's enterprise
in Barbados and a similar venture of his in Antigua
provided the only bright spots in the whole field of
missionary activity for slaves throughout the British
colonies in the Caribbean.

The slaves were accustomed to have Sundays free and
usually spent their day of rest doing certain essential jobs
for themselves. It was, therefore, difficult for them to find
time on Sundays to be instructed in the Christian Gospel.
To meet this difficulty the rule was made that on the

Codrington plantations the slaves should have Saturday afternoons for themselves and on Sundays they were required to attend religious instruction.

The vision of Christopher Codrington and the work on his plantations were extremely important because they prepared the way for the eventual abolition of slavery. Codrington was the first man in the British Caribbean to emphasize the view that the slave was a person and not merely a piece of property. It is true that the Codrington plantations were worked by slaves. But this must be judged in the light of the ideas of the time. No one at that period seemed to think that sugar could be produced except by slave labour.

The significance of the Codrington experiment was not that his estates owned slaves, but that the managers were instructed to give them the benefits of education and the consolations of the Christian religion. The important thing was not that Codrington's agents ran the plantations with slave labour, but that they made their slaves members of the Christian society and thus endowed them, as it were, with the status of spiritual equality.

It may be difficult for us at the present time to understand how radical and far-reaching were the ideas of Christopher Codrington. The slave-owners who opposed him constantly expressed the fear that to baptize and instruct the slaves were the first steps along the road to freedom. And that is exactly how it turned out. Once the enslaved African was granted an immortal soul, his right to physical liberty could not be denied him for long.

Codrington persuaded some of the men of his time in the Caribbean to accept the opinion that a slave should be a Christian and this led, within the next hundred years, to the revolutionary view that slavery was contrary to the principles of the Christian religion because all men were the sons of God.

The Campaign for Freedom

The idea that slavery itself was unchristian was taken up by the Wesleyans and other Nonconformist bodies who sent missionaries out to the West Indies. The campaign launched by the Evangelical churches went hand in hand with the ideas liberated by the French Revolution. Liberty, Equality and Fraternity were slogans that affected the West Indies as much as they affected other parts of the world, and all this had a decisive influence on the anti-slavery campaign which started in England and spread to the Caribbean.

The campaign for emancipation will always be associated with such names as Thomas Clarkson and Granville Sharp, William Wilberforce and Thomas Fowell Buxton. But in the West Indies we should remember such men as William Knibb and Moses Barker in Jamaica and Bussa and Washington Franklin in Barbados, who led the 1816 slave insurrection.

It was largely due to the efforts of the English agitators that the slave trade was abolished in 1807. This act made it illegal for anyone to import slaves into the British colonies. The next step was to make sure that slaves were not smuggled from Africa to the West Indies and for this purpose a Slave Registry Act was passed by the British Parliament, Wilberforce being its most eloquent spokesman in the House of Commons.

The planters of Barbados could see the writing plainly on the wall. They knew that, once the slave trade was abolished, the next attack would be on the whole system of slavery itself. The abolition of slavery, they felt, would knock the bottom out of their world.

But the planters were tough and tenacious men. When the Slave Registry Bill was first proposed, they launched a vigorous counter-attack. They declared that they were not opposed to the Bill in principle but they strongly objected to the proposal that the Imperial Government should impose a tax on the slave-owners in the colonies to carry the measure into effect. Once again, the House of Assembly, as in the days of the early settlement, raised the cry of 'No taxation without representation' and they solemnly reminded the British Government that the revolt of the American Colonies was caused by a similar attempt to establish this obnoxious doctrine.

So spirited was the opposition of the Assembly that the slaves began to believe that the Slave Registry Bill meant more than it really did. They imagined that England wanted to give them their freedom and that the planters were keeping them from it. As a result, there was a formidable insurrection in 1816, with Washington Franklin, a free mulatto, as its intellectual leader and Bussa, an African, as the commander in the field. The

William Wilberforce

revolt was soon quelled, however, owing to the strength of the militia which was powerfully aided by regular troops.

The End of Slavery

After the final defeat of Napoleon, the English abolitionists were able once again to occupy the centre of the stage in public affairs. The pressure for emancipation kept increasing, with Wilberforce and Buxton taking the lead. But there were other forces behind the campaign besides the missionaries in the West Indies and the agitators in England. While the abolitionists urged that slavery was unchristian, there were other learned men who said that it was wasteful and inefficient.

England was undergoing a great change at the time and its large-scale industries were looking not merely to the West Indies but to the larger markets of the world. The West Indian market was too small to occupy the whole attention of the English manufacturer.

It was felt that the British West Indies could no longer compete on equal terms with such places as Cuba and the East Indies, and that West Indian sugar should not continue to enjoy a monopoly of the English market because it was too expensive. Thus it came to pass that both the economists and the abolitionists seemed to be arguing for the same thing — the abolition of slavery in the West Indies and the overthrow of the West Indian sugar monopoly.

The battle waged by the planters in Barbados and the

other British colonies was, therefore, a hopeless one. They were fighting a lost cause and powerful forces of the nineteenth century were arrayed solidly against them. In vain did they try to postpone the inevitable by improving the lot of the slaves. They granted them the legal protection they were denied in earlier years. Whereas the killing of a slave, in former times, was regarded as a minor offence punishable only by a fine of £15, it was now legally defined as murder. Efforts were made to lower the high mortality among the slaves, to lift the number of births over the number of deaths, so that no one would be tempted to break the law by smuggling new slaves from Africa. And steps were taken to improve the living and working conditions of the slaves.

In spite of this programme of reform, it was plain that the institution of slavery was doomed. In 1833 the British Parliament finally decided the issue by passing the Emancipation Act and on August 1st of the following year the slaves were declared to be free throughout the British colonies.

Further Reading

The West Indies Before and After Emancipation by John Davy.
Christopher Codrington by Vincent T. Harlow.
The Church in the West Indies by A. Caldecott.

Chapter 14

THE NEW ORDER

IN spite of what we said at the end of the last chapter, the slaves were not given their complete freedom on August 1st, 1834. The Colonial Office realised that the change from slavery to freedom would be difficult and it was therefore decided that there should be a period of apprenticeship during which the Negroes would continue to work for the plantations as before. The planters, as in the days of slavery, would provide the slaves with the necessities of life and the Negroes would give them their labour without payment for three-quarters of the week. The idea behind the system of apprenticeship may have been a good one. It was thought that there might have been trouble after emancipation since neither planters nor ex-slaves were accustomed to the conditions of freedom. It was feared that there would be a period of unrest during which the plantations would not be properly looked after and the economic condition of the colonies would suffer.

As it was, the system of apprenticeship did not work satisfactorily and Barbados decided to put an end to it on August 1st, 1838. The slaves were given their full freedom on that date and the island set to working out its destiny as a free society.

It should always be remembered to the credit of our ancestors that Barbados gave the vote to the free coloured people in 1831 and saved them by law from all civil and military discrimination. This section of Barbadian society had grown steadily during the years before emancipation. It consisted of former slaves who had been freed by their masters or had purchased their freedom under special circumstances; of slave concubines and their mulatto children who had gained their liberty through the grateful generosity of their owners; of worn-out slaves who had grown too old to be of any economic value and had been turned out of the plantations; of favourite slaves who had been liberated by special clauses in the wills of their former masters.

When the slaves were freed, they received the same benefits that the free coloured people had enjoyed before them and in the eyes of the law they were thus the equals of all other citizens. It was in these circumstances that the task of building the new order of society was begun. The population of the island was then 103,007 and there were indications that it was rapidly increasing. Of this total, 14,959 were whites, 5,146 were mixed and 82,902 were Negroes.

Adjusting to the Change

It had been feared that, when slavery was abolished, there would be a disturbed period of riots and civil commotion. Actually, emancipation came to Barbados much more smoothly and peacefully than most people had expected. Much of the credit for this must be given to the Anglican Church.

At one time, as we said in an earlier chapter, the Church of England had left the missionary work among the slaves almost entirely to the Nonconformists. But, a few years before emancipation, the Church saw the needs of the time and sent out Bishop Coleridge to Barbados. Under his leadership, the Anglican Church played a great part in preparing the island for the great social changes that were to come when the slaves were freed.

Many people said that emancipation would bring a train of evils upon Barbados. It was predicted that the abolition of slavery would be as great a disaster as the terrible hurricane of 1831; that the cost of producing sugar would go up; that the amount of sugar produced would go down; that the slaves would refuse to work after freedom had been granted to them; that the white population would emigrate to other countries in large numbers, as they had done some two hundred years before when sugar and African slavery were introduced into the island.

But none of these things happened in Barbados. It is quite true that in most of the other colonies the end of the old order meant the complete overthrow of the planter class. But that was certainly not the case in Barbados. This island differed from Jamaica, for instance, in at least one important respect. In Jamaica most of the plantation owners were absentee landlords — men who lived in England — but in Barbados a considerable number of estates were owned by local whites.

These owners continued to live in Barbados after

William Hart Coleridge

emancipation. They were tough, self-reliant men and succeeded in adjusting themselves to the new order of society. They were not daunted by the changed circumstances of the island after 1838 and they managed to keep the plantations well supplied with labour.

The planters of Barbados were helped by a number of factors. First, the British Government granted them over one and a half millions sterling as compensation for the financial loss they had incurred through the emancipation of the slaves. This represented an average of approximately £20 per slave and, though it was less than the cost of an able-bodied slave at the time, it should be remembered that the compensation was paid on the basis of all slaves of ages ranging from less than one year to over 100 years. Certainly, the British grant was a substantial one and helped the planters to adjust themselves to the new order of society.

Another factor was that the Mother Country relieved them of the 4½ per cent duty with which the island had been burdened for nearly two hundred years. In addition, Barbados adopted the 'located labourers' system which we shall now try to explain.

After emancipation the former slaves were left in their houses and allotments and, in return for this benefit, they were required to give their labour to the plantations concerned at reduced wages. If the 'located labourer', as he was called, refused to give his services on these terms, he could be ejected from his house and land and the crops he had grown on his allotment could be taken over at what was generally less than their current value. If the located labourer left of his own accord, seeking higher wages on another plantation, his crops were taken over without any compensation at all. It is true that the power of ejection was not frequently exercised, since nothing would have been more calculated to produce ill-will between employers and employees, but the possibility of its enforcement assured the planters of a continuous supply of labour.

The located labourers system succeeded in maintaining the efficiency of the plantations after emancipation. But perhaps the greatest advantage which the planters in Barbados enjoyed was that there were no vacant lands on which the ex-slaves could settle as independent farmers instead of remaining on the plantations. In Jamaica, Trinidad and Guyana, the situation was quite different. In those territories there were uncultivated lands in the hills and the bush where the newly eman-cipated could establish themselves, away from the unhappy memories of the sugar estate. But in Barbados, as in Antigua and St. Kitts, the ex-slaves had no such opportunities and they were forced to continue with their work on the plantations in order to gain a livelihood.

The Threat from Slave Sugar

In these circumstances, and with the planters forming a well organised group, who were always on the lookout for improved methods of production, it was natural that the island should fare better than most of the other colonies.

Indeed, within a few years after emancipation, the sugar plantations were being run as efficiently as ever and at one time the production of sugar was greater than in the period shortly before slavery was abolished.

But the courage of the planters and the industry of the ex-slaves were soon to be threatened from outside. At one time Barbados could be certain of a market in England for her sugar. Countries like Brazil and Cuba could afford to produce cheaper sugar because they still employed slave labour. But England protected Barbados and the other British colonies by making the duty on foreign sugar greater than on colonial sugar. England was being pressed at this time, however, to adopt a policy of free trade and in due course she decided to make the duties on foreign and colonial sugar equal.

You may imagine the feelings of the planters when this happened. They knew that they could not compete with countries which still employed slave labour and they felt that the Mother Country had betrayed them. Faced with this situation, Barbados did what other colonies did. It cut down expenses by reducing the wages of the workers. As a result, the labourers were unable to provide themselves with the necessities of life and their standard of living fell to a dangerously low level. Moreover, the island, with its reduced income, was unable to provide the social services that were essential and it is therefore not surprising that Barbados went through a dismal period when epidemic followed epidemic, taking a heavy toll of human life. The worst of these was the cholera epidemic of 1854, of which many unhappy stories have been handed down from one generation to the other to the present day.

Forming a Society

On the whole, however, it may be said that the history of Barbados was more stable than that of most of the other colonies. I have already given you the reasons for this. But I should mention, in addition, the quality of the leadership with which the island was blessed during this critical period. She had leaders such as Sir Robert Bowcher Clarke, a white Barbadian, who persuaded the planters to think not only of themselves but of the island as a whole, and Samuel Jackman Prescod, a mulatto, who prepared the coloured people to play their part in the difficult business of self-government.

If Barbados owes a great deal to Clarke, it owes an equal, if not greater, debt to Prescod. The latter believed passionately in the virtues of parliamentary government. He regarded it as his special mission to persuade his large following of black and coloured people that they must look for their salvation to no one but themselves.

He succeeded in inspiring the emancipated classes and the Barbadians of mixed European and African origin with the feeling that they should take as much pride in the business of self-government as the early settlers of the island. It was largely due to Prescod's work that a sense of community was developed among the various sections of the island's people and that a growing body of opinion became strongly attached to representative institutions.

In this way Barbados succeeded, to some extent, in bringing all classes to realise that their salvation lay in changing the island from a group of hostile sections into a community of men who were vitally interested in the general welfare.

Clearly, the leaders of Barbados accepted the idea that the great task of the time was not merely to free a race but to form a society. They realised that their main duty was not only to emancipate the slaves but to integrate them into a new order of society.

Further Reading

Barbados Diocesan History
    edited by J. E. Reece and C. G. Clarke-Hunt.
The British West Indies by W. L. Burn.

Chapter 15

THE FEDERATION RIOTS

I T is unfortunate for the peace of the island that Barbados did not keep up the good work it had started just before and after emancipation. The great efforts that had been made by Bishop Coleridge, by Clarke and by Prescod to bring the different classes of Barbadian society together were not continued and before long Barbados began to drift down the slippery slope that leads to revolution.

The underlying cause of the trouble lay in the declining prosperity of the island. Several countries had begun to produce beet sugar and the Governments of those countries paid large sums of money to help with the cost of production. In the last chapter we explained how the planters felt when the Mother Country imported sugar from places that still employed slave labour. Now their complaint was that England bought beet sugar from Europe and that the West Indies could not compete with the beet sugar producers and were therefore bound to lose money.

Since beet sugar could be sold to England cheaper than West Indian sugar, the planters of Barbados were forced to lower their prices. Soon they were struggling, sometimes almost hopelessly, to keep out of debt. They began to owe more and more money to people in England who helped to finance the plantations. More estates passed from Barbadian into English hands, while those planters who kept their heads above water felt it necessary to economise in whatever way they could.

The Seed of Unrest

It was this that sowed the seed of unrest in the island. One of the most tempting ways to cut down expenses was to reduce the wages of the sugar labourers and that is exactly what the planters did. Stern measures were taken to ensure an adequate supply of labour for the estates. Labourers who occupied land belonging to the plantations were required to give their labour in return at lower wages than they could obtain outside. If they resisted, they were made to quit the plantation lands without notice and their crops were taken over without proper appraisal. The system of 'located labourers' thus became more and more unpopular.

Moreover, during these grim years the planters did what they could to avoid taxation. There was little money, therefore, for social services. Little was done to provide poor relief, or to look after those who were ill in body or mind. Emigration was not encouraged. Crime, usually the result of hunger and privation, began to grow, the poor could not pay their debts and the prison was filled with people.

The Colonial Office was not satisfied with what was happening in Barbados. It thought that more could be done for the poor people, in spite of the hard times the island was going through. It felt that the island would be better governed if the House of Assembly was abolished and the Mother Country took the government of Barbados into its hands. The plan it had in mind was that Barbados should be united with the Windward Islands and a Crown Colony system established to govern the proposed federation.

The Governor who was sent out to carry this plan into effect was John Pope-Hennessy. He was an Irishman, with a strong passion for helping the underdog. He felt very sorry for the poor people of the island and frequently called attention to their needs. He explained the federal plan as something that would give the labourers a chance to emigrate to the neighbouring colonies and improve their lot. The mass of the people looked on the Governor as their friend and felt God had sent him to help them.

The Federal Plan
But the rest of the island — the planters, the merchants and the white and coloured middle classes — did not like the federal plan at all. They wanted to keep the House of Assembly, which had now been going for nearly two hundred and fifty years, and they combined to oppose the Colonial Office.

As the months went by, the situation became very tense. The planters and their supporters opposed the federal plan with increasing bitterness and the Negro masses became increasingly anxious to see it accepted. There was a great deal of misunderstanding on both sides and things moved rapidly to a climax until April 1876, when an explosion of violence took place in the island.

The trouble started at Byde Mill plantation in St. George, when two men entered the estate yard, one holding a red flag and the other waving a sword. They asked for a drink and then blew a conch shell which seemed to be the signal for the labourers to raid the potato fields. After this, there began a campaign of riot and plunder which spread to various parts of the island, but the amazing thing was that the lawbreakers felt they had the blessing of the Governor.

Plantation houses were attacked, cattle wounded or maimed, crops destroyed or taken away. There was little threat to human life because the rioters believed that the Governor had given them permission to take things for themselves but not to shed blood. Still, the situation looked very ugly at times and those who opposed the federal plan left the country areas and took refuge in the military buildings around the Garrison Savannah and in the ships at anchor in Carlisle Bay.

Pope-Hennessy worked unwearyingly to remove the tragic misunderstanding of his policy and after a few days the uprising was quelled. Then the planters and their supporters counter-attacked vigorously. They blamed the Governor for the riots and they asked the Secretary of State for the Colonies to recall him.

Pope-Hennessy remained in Barbados for a while but relations between him and the House of Assembly became so difficult that the Colonial Office eight months later removed him from the island and transferred him to Hong Kong.

Conrad Reeves

The man who led the House of Assembly to victory against the Colonial Office was W. C. (later Sir Conrad) Reeves, a coloured lawyer, who later rose to become the first Chief Justice of his race in the British Empire. He was enthusiastically supported by the planters and merchants and the white and coloured middle class, who were determined to preserve the island's system of government.

Reeves saw the nature of the struggle more clearly perhaps than anyone else in Barbados. He knew that the quarrel between Barbados and the Colonial Office could not be settled unless there was some compromise by both sides. He realised that the Colonial Office would leave the island's constitution alone, if Barbados agreed to put its house in order.

Mainly as a result of Reeve's leadership, several important things were done. The Executive Committee system was adopted in 1881 to make the island's system of government more efficient. The franchise was lowered three years later so that more people than before would be able to vote. The facilities for education were increased and certain measures were passed to improve the lot of the 'located labourers' and to better the conditions of the poor. By doing these things, Barbados persuaded the Mother Country that she could be trusted with the representative institutions which she had enjoyed from the beginning of her history.

At the entrance of the House of Assembly you can still

Sir William Conrad Reeves, Chief Justice, 1886–1902

see the statue of Reeves which was erected by his fellow-countrymen to honour his services during the Federation crisis. It is the only statue of its kind in the island. In his day, Reeves, though idolised by the upper and middle classes of Barbados, was regarded by the mass of the people as a traitor to his race. But as the years went by, it became increasingly clear that Reeves, like his predecessor Prescod, stood for an important idea — that the people of Barbados, of what ever class or colour, should work together to show that they were capable of running a representative system of government.

Further Reading

The History, Civil and Commercial, of the British Colonies in the West Indies by Bryan Edwards.
Barbados and the Federation Question 1871—1885 by Bruce Hamilton.
The British Empire in America by John Oldmixon.
Verandah by James Pope-Hennessy.

Chapter 16

OUT OF THE GLOOM

AFTER the crisis of 1876, Barbados entered into a gloomy period of its economic life. It was an era of acute depression but it will cheer you to consider the heroic efforts made by the Barbadians to meet the difficulties of the time.

The island had to pass through one ordeal after another and at times the prospects of recovery must have daunted the faint of heart. Yet Barbados produced men who were able to guide the island during this critical period and to lay the foundation for its development and welfare in the years to come.

The first major problem arose through the increased competition from beet sugar. Because of the bounties paid to help the export of this product the West Indies were totally unable to compete with the countries of Europe that were producing beet sugar. Prices fell rapidly and the value of plantations in Barbados declined year after year.

But that was not the worst of it. The island experienced several years of drought that seriously reduced the size of the sugar crop and, in addition, a strange disease began to attack the roots and stems of the Bourbon cane on which the sugar industry of the island depended.

The man who saved Barbados from complete ruin was John Redmond Bovell. Working with J. B. Harrison, then Island Professor of Chemistry, he carried out several experiments on the effects of manures. At a time when the courage of planters was beginning to fail Bovell and Harrison showed them the value of artificial fertilisers. By following their advice, the planters were able to increase their crops and they began to see that their hope for the future lay in scientific research.

Then Bovell saw another opportunity to serve his native land at a time of great peril. Since the Bourbon cane was failing, he realised that an alternative cane would have to be found as a source of sugar supply. Here again, he worked with Harrison. A number of experiments were carried out and the success of their work helped not only Barbados but all the countries of the world that had previously depended on the Bourbon cane.

Joseph Chamberlain

In spite of all these efforts, however, the island was still faced with her gravest problem. All she did to improve her sugar industry and to make it more resistant to disease and insects did not remove the greatest obstacle to her recovery. So long as the countries of Europe subsidised beet sugar and so long as England bought it without import duties, there seemed to be no hope for the West Indies.

Barbados had increased her crops by using proper manures. She had solved the problem of supply by raising new varieties of sugar cane from seed, but nothing could be done about the threat from beet sugar unless she received help from outside.

It was in these circumstances that Joseph Chamberlain became Secretary of State for the Colonies. He was determined to save the sugar industry of the West Indies from bankruptcy. A Royal Commission was appointed in 1896 to go into the whole question and the recommendations it submitted in the following year were to play a great part in the recovery of the West Indies.

Chamberlain persuaded the British Government to help the colonies over the crisis by granting them considerable sums of money. He urged that the question of beet sugar bounties should be discussed at an international level and it was largely due to his persistence that the Brussels Conference in 1903 agreed to abolish the bounty system.

The debt that Barbados owes to Joseph Chamberlain is a very great one. The next time you go over the 'swing' bridge, you should call to mind why the Barbadians named it after the great Colonial Secretary.

Patriot and Statesman
Barbados could scarcely have survived the ups and downs of this period unless she was governed by one of the greatest statesmen in her history. The man who guided Barbados safely through the ever-recurring crises of those years was Sir Herbert Greaves, a white man, whose disinterested patriotism entitles him to the respect of all classes and sections of the island

If you have followed this narrative carefully up to this point, you will come to one quite definite conclusion. And that is that a Barbadian of outstanding character and ability has always come forward to save his country when its fortunes appear to be at their lowest ebb.

In the darkest days of slavery, Christopher Codrington, a white Barbadian, prepared the way for the freedom of the slaves by putting into practice the principles of Christianity. Samuel Jackman Prescod, a mulatto, vindicated, in the years following emancipation, the right of the black and mixed people to share in the business of self-government. Conrad Reeves, a coloured Barbadian, in the great battle with the Colonial Office, had fought for the principle that the community, with all its varying sections, should have the power to handle its own affairs.

Sir Herbert Greaves

And now Greaves showed that Barbados, which had recently preserved the right to govern itself, had the ability to save itself from the perils that surrounded it. As Attorney General of Barbados, he led the House of Assembly with a firm hand and kept the island on an even keel. He inspired his countrymen with the courage to bear their trials with a high spirit and with the vision to plan for the future with confidence.

The grant given to Barbados by the British Government was £80,000. Greaves would not allow this money to be distributed among planters who had suffered heavy losses during the crisis, for he knew that it would soon be all spent and that no permanent benefit would accrue to the island. Instead, it was used as the capital of the Sugar Industry Agricultural Bank, an institution that proved a sheet anchor for the sugar industry in the years that lay ahead.

It is to Greaves's lasting credit that this Bank was established as a public institution which lent the planters money to improve their machinery or to finance their crops. In other colonies, the British Government grants were soon spent, but the Sugar Industry Agricultural Bank still stands to-day as a monument to the generosity of the British taxpayer and to the statesmanship of Sir Herbert Greaves.

Our Water Supply

Another great service which Greaves performed was that he persuaded the Barbadians, in their years of endurance, to improve the water supply of the island. The poor people at the time obtained their water from ponds and shallow wells and the upper classes from deeper wells and rain water tanks. You may imagine how the people suffered when a large number of ponds dried up owing to several years of drought.

Bridgetown was scarcely better off than other parts of the island. Many people obtained drinking water from

Beckles Spring on the Bay Estate. The owner of this spring must have done a considerable trade since he sold large quantities of water to retailers who then sold it to the people at ten cents for four gallons.

A big step was taken before Greaves's time, when a private company was formed to improve the water system. That was in 1859 and the company was guaranteed a government subsidy on condition that it gave Bridgetown a daily supply of half a million gallons of pure water. Though this undertaking was not completely fulfilled, it brought about a great improvement for Bridgetown.

But the people of the country districts still depended on wells and ponds and Greaves realised that a far-reaching scheme would have to be adopted to make the water supply more satsifactory. The fact that people drank impure water was probably a contributory cause to the epidemics of typhoid, dysentry and other water-borne diseases which plagued the island from time to time.

Plans were, therefore, drawn up to improve the water supply not only for Bridgetown but for the rural areas of Barbados. The idea was to supply all parts of the island rising as high as 175 feet above sea-level and to bring an abundant supply of water to the poor by means of four hundred free public taps, each of them providing about five thousand gallons a day.

To carry out this programme, another private company was formed and a project started to intercept some of the island's underground streams, build tunnels to bring this water to the surface at different points and from these points to distribute the water to all places at lower levels.

Bold Action

Barbados now had two private water companies, one supplying Bridgetown and the other the rural areas. Greaves considered that the rivalry between the two companies was not in the best interests of the island and in 1895 he persuaded the Legislature to buy both of them and establish a Government Waterworks Department.

The new waterworks department used the sources of water that had been used by the two private companies — Newcastle Spring, Codrington College Spring and Bowmanston Pumping Station, Harrison Cave, Baker's Cave, Cole's Cave and Plumtree Gully. The plans of the two companies were taken over by the Government and since then there has been remarkable progress in the task of providing a pure and ample water supply for the people of Barbados.

As more became known of the island's geological structure the water system could be planned more scientifically. It was discovered that the entire coral-rock formation of the island was a sort of sieve or drip-stone. Rain water passed through the coral rock and dripped downwards through the fine pores and larger openings under the natural influence of gravity.

When the water reached the bottom of the coral-rock, it was held up by the underlying stratum of impervious material and, as a result, large quantities of 'sheet water' were stored in the coral. Below the St. George's Valley, for instance, there is the greatest reservoir of pure, fresh water in the island.

Moreover, it became known not only that the porous coral-rock was full of the finest quality of fresh water, but that, near the coast, this water was held back in the land by the sea.

This is a curious fact which you may want explained. The sea water acts as a barrier to the fresh water because it is heavier — because it has a higher specific gravity. Since the fresh water is dammed up in this way, it can rise in the island's underground reservoirs until it stands at sea-level.

Sometimes when you visit Fresh Water Bay, you may see fresh water flowing freely at the sea shore. This happens when the tide is low. For the barrier formed by the sea water is then lowered and allows some of the fresh water which has been stored up to escape on to the beach. I should add that such off-shore springs are numerous all around the limestone part of the island.

Under Greaves's leadership, the island started the system of free public taps and to-day two-thirds of the island's population obtain free water from roadside stand-posts. The daily water supply has increased to nearly seven million gallons. Most of this is pumped from the coral-rock at sea-level but a large portion is also drawn from natural springs and from an underground spring at Bowmanston.

Recently an underground lake, called Sweet Vale, has been discovered about 150 feet below the island's surface and it is hoped that this will solve the problem we have to face when the subterranean stream at Bowmanston becomes turbid after heavy rainfall. Another improvement to which we may perhaps look forward is indicated by the research now being undertaken on the possibility of obtaining water for irrigation purposes.

Barbados has reason to be proud of its public water supply system and, while we must always be thankful to the scientists and technicians who worked to bring it to its present position, we should ever remember the services rendered by Greaves in this field in a critical period of the island's fortunes.

Further Reading

Report of the British Union Company on Geological Investigations of the Ground Water Resources of Barbados, B.W.I.
by Alfred Senn.
Our Common Heritage by F. A. Hoyos.

Chapter 17

THE TRIUMPH OF CHARACTER

IN an earlier chapter of this book you have read of the trials through which Barbadians passed during the latter part of the nineteenth century. They had to face the hazards of drought and depression, of storm and subsidised beet sugar, of Bourbon cane disease and the instability of a one-crop economy.

Yet, as the island moved towards the twentieth century, it seemed as if the fates were resolved to test even further the courage and endurance of the Barbadians. The hurricane of 1898 had damaged the island's water supply and caused serious outbreaks of typhoid and dysentry. And, two years after the century began, Barbados was visited by the much dreaded disease of smallpox.

Nor was this the end of the tribulations the island had to endure. In 1906 the Imperial Troops, which had long been stationed in Barbados, were withdrawn. This was a heavy blow for those whose social life drew much of its colour and gaiety from the presence of the military. But it was an even heavier loss to the island as a whole, for the Imperial Troops used to contribute some £80,000 a year to the national income of Barbados.

In 1908, however, the island, which had not yet recovered from the terrible ravages of smallpox, was visited by an even more dreadful scourge, an epidemic of yellow fever. Even then there were more trials in store for the sorely-tested Barbadians. The years 1911, 1912 and 1914 brought with them periods of severe drought and the suffering and privation of those times can well be imagined. In the words of a popular story at the time, 'Hunger' and 'Nakedness', symbolised by two gaunt figures, were the constant companions of the poor people in the island.

When everything seemed to be going against them, the Barbadians showed once again that they possessed the necessary character to overcome their misfortunes. It was heartening to see the undaunted and resourceful spirit with which all sections of the population, white, black and coloured, fought to save themselves from despair and ruin. Even more encouraging it was to see that the islanders, led by men like Sir William Chandler and Sir Charles Pitcher Clarke, were resolved to demonstrate that, in spite of every calamity, they were capable of managing their own affairs without aid or interference from the Colonial Office.

One of the causes of their survival may well be that they never lost their sense of balance and their zest for life. All Barbadians show a keen interest in music — from the highest in the land to the humble village choirs which made themselves great favourites at Christmas time. And, with the visits of English teams and the beginning of intercolonial tournaments in 1901, cricket rapidly became a unifying influence that enabled all sections of the community to find a happy release from the strain of those arduous years.

The Search for More Income

There was at least one lesson that the Barbadians had learnt during the agony of the late nineteenth century. They now knew it would be dangerous, if not fatal, to rely on the sugar industry as their only means of support. If the promise of a new era was to be fulfilled, they realised they would have to look about for new ways to make a living.

The sugar industry was not, of course, to be abandoned. With the uncertainties of the world market, it was an uphill struggle to keep the industry going. Though the prospects at times looked bleak, the planters held on tenaciously and worked unceasingly to improve their methods of production. But the absentee owners could not stand the strain. They began to grow panicky and, one after the other, their plantations were sold to local men who readily bought them up.

Thus it was that most of the sugar estates in the island passed once again into Barbadian hands. The white Barbadians of the twentieth century had inherited the qualities of the planters of old. They shared their faith in the land and their confidence in the sugar industry. They knew that sugar was the ideal crop because of the island's sunshine, its moderate rainfall, its coral soil, its system of drainage, its wind-swept climate and its large labour force.

But the Barbadians were determined to find other sources of revenue. In 1903 a trial shipment of fancy molasses, manufactured at Rugby Plantation, in St.

Thomas, was sent to Canada. This type of molasses was made by using the entire cane juice without removing any of the sugar content. Happily, this experiment was well received in Canada and from it was born an industry that has brought a great deal of money to the island.

It is of interest to know that the manufacture of fancy molasses kept the windmill plants going in Barbados for a much longer time than might have been the case without this industry. While Puerto Rico, our chief competitor, went in for large central factories, Barbados discovered that small plants were more suitable for the production of fancy molasses. That is why the windmills remained in existence in the island up to recent times. But, one by one, they were forced to close down owing to the rising cost of production and you may know that the last windmill of them all was finally dismantled at Colleton, St. Peter, in 1946.

Several attempts were made to grow crops to take the place of sugar but these were not successful. However, the Barbadians were not daunted in their search for additional sources of income, and the early twentieth century saw quite a successful revival of the sea island cotton industry. The Government took active measures to encourage the growth of cotton and the planters readily responded because they knew it was a crop that suited the drier parts of the island.

Persistence Rewarded

In their search for new ways of making a living, the

Barbadians discovered that the island's natural advantages made it a fine resort for visitors from overseas. As early as 1887, the Marine and the Crane Hotels had been built and, as the twentieth century proceeded on its course, more accommodation was provided for visitors from North America and from the Mother Country. In addition, houses were rented at the seaside, particularly at Worthing, to the many South Americans who came to the island. The reason for all this activity to satisfy the visitors is easily understood. The Barbadians had realised that tourism was the sort of enterprise that would benefit

The Colonnade at the Turn of the Century

all classes and sections of the island's community.

But perhaps the greatest source of income to the island came from the opportunities offered by emigration. In the past, it had been the white Barbadians who emigrated and most of them never returned to the island. But the emigration of the early twentieth century was quite a different matter. For the first time in their history, black and mixed Barbadians had the chance to emigrate in large numbers and they went to the neighbouring lands in the Caribbean, to the U.S.A., to Brazil and to Panama.

The important thing about this exodus was that the emigrants kept in touch with their relatives at home and sent back substantial sums of money. Large remittances came to Barbados in a steady stream from the U.S.A. and Brazil, but it was Panama that proved the greatest source of income to the island. In the first decade of the twentieth century, some 20,000 men went to Panama and these sent back something like a quarter of a million dollars a year to their hard-pressed families in Barbados.

In due course, this money from the emigrants was to produce far-reaching social results in the island. For their relatives at home used a great deal of this 'Panama money', as it was called, to buy little plots of land when certain plantations were cut up and sold. From this was started that 'silent revolution', through which, as the years went by, one-fifth of the island's arable land passed into the hands of peasants and small-holders.

Barbados had reason to be grateful to those countries which opened their doors to her citizens of all classes and which liberally made use of their industry in the early twentieth century.

Thus you see how the Barbadians, by dint of hard work and enterprise, managed to overcome their troubles. And before long, fortune herself began to help them in their strenuous efforts to lift themselves out of their troubles. During the first World War of 1914–18 many countries of Europe were over-run by military forces and the sugar beet fields, which had once competed so disastrously with West Indian sugar plantations, were destroyed. This gave Barbados its great chance and the sugar industry soared to a level of prosperity it had rarely attained before.

Nature also decided to reward the Barbadians for their perseverance and the rain, falling in large quantities, gave them large crops at a time when prices were unusually high. Plantations that were heavily in debt before were able to pay off what they owed and the planters were wise enough to use much of their big profits to buy improved machinery. It was small wonder that the island felt that its years of suffering had not been in vain.

Further Reading

The Fall of the Planter Class in the British Caribbean
    by L. J. Ragatz.
The Economic Geography of Barbados by Otis P. Starkey.

Chapter 18

TOWARDS STABILITY

I T was not to be expected that the war-time boom, which brought great prosperity to Barbados, would last indefinitely. One unhappy result of this prosperity was that the cotton industry suffered, since much of the land used for cotton growing was given over to sugar. Barbados once again became dangerously dependent on sugar and, as a war-time measure, a law had to be passed compelling the planters to grow ground provisions to safeguard the island's food supply.

Two years after the war ended, the price of sugar fell with a crash. The island's staple product could only fetch one-sixth of the price it reached at the time of the boom and in 1921 the price fell even lower. This was a heavy blow to the island and the Government was unable to raise money to pay its expenses. It was to meet this urgent need that Income Tax was introduced into the island in 1921.

Thanks to good rainfall, improved cultivation and a slight increase in the price of sugar, Barbados was saved from almost certain ruin. Yet her condition still remained serious. It was felt that alternative crops could not be grown with such success as to take the place of sugar. A Royal Commission, appointed in 1938 and reporting in 1940, declared that the island would never be sure of its future unless the Mother Country kept the price of West

Indian sugar at a satisfactory level by increasing the protective tariff which was called the Imperial Preference.

It was in these circumstances that the democratic movement was launched in the island by Charles Duncan O'Neale in 1924. The leader of this movement pointed out that during the boom caused by the First World War the labouring population had shared little in the prosperity of the sugar industry, and he stressed that in time of depression the working classes felt the pinch more acutely than any other section of the community. Coming at a time when the post-war ferment was giving rise to liberal ideas in many countries of the world, O'Neale's Democratic League met with widespread support and enthusiasm in the island during the 1920s and early 1930s.

The Hungry Thirties

But, as the years went by, the situation in Barbados seemed to get worse rather than better. During the trying period at the beginning of the twentieth century, thousands of Barbadians, who were hard-pressed at home, had been able to emigrate to various parts of the world, to improve their fortunes and provide relief for their relatives in Barbados. But the depressed condition of the entire world in 1929 offered the Barbadians no such hope of relief. The countries which had formerly taken them into their midst were no longer prepared to receive them, and to make matters worse, the emigrants of earlier years now returned to increase the pressure on the resources of the hard-hit island.

Barbados now entered into what may be called the 'Hungry Thirties' of the present century. The other islands of the West Indies also suffered from falling prices and the unhappy condition of the world. But it may perhaps be said that Barbados, with its teeming population and its limited resources, suffered as much as, if not more than, its neighbours in the Caribbean.

It is not surprising that discontent and unrest began to show themselves up and down the Caribbean. Soon the spark of revolt leapt from colony to colony and before long Barbados followed the example of other restless spirits in the West Indies. For in July 1937 labour disturbances occurred in the island and 14 persons were killed and 47 wounded before law and order were restored.

Out of the seething unrest of that period was born the Barbados Progressive League under the leadership first of the late C. E. Braithwaite and then of G. H. (now Sir Grantley) Adams. With its two offspring, the Barbados Labour Party and the Barbados Workers' Union, the League was to play a momentous part in the political and industrial life of the island. It took up the cause of the underprivileged which had been championed by the Democratic League during the preceding decade and fought to promote the ends of justice, to bring about industrial peace and to provide the island with a happy measure of stability.

Development of Parties
The lowering of the franchise in 1944 had a significant

effect on the politics of the island. In the elections held in that year, with artisans and agricultural labourers voting for the first time, three political parties each won eight of the twenty-four seats in the House of Assembly. These were the Barbados Labour Party, led by Grantley Adams, the Congress Party, led by W. A. Crawford and advocating a reform programme similar to that of the Labour Party, and the Conservative Electors' Association, led first by J. H. Wilkinson and later by Ernest D. Mottley.

Two years later, the Bushe Experiment was introduced. It was a notable change in the island's constitutional

Sir Grantley Adams

procedure. Under the Experiment, the majority leader in the House of Assembly would select the four House members who were members of the Executive Committee. Those members would be in charge of the general policy relating to Government Departments and would be responsible for the affairs of those Departments both in the Executive Committee and in the House of Assembly. The Executive Committee would now no longer be a collection of individuals, selected to advise the Governor, but an effective organ of government remaining in power so long as it retained the confidence of the House. The Attorney General would lose the traditional role he had played as the Leader of the House and the majority leader would head the government virtually as Premier.

It is small wonder that the elections of 1946 were fought with intense rivalry. The Barbados Labour Party won nine seats, the Electors' Association eight and the Congress Party seven. These results made an alliance between Adams and Crawford inevitable and a coalition government was formed, with the leader of the Labour Party selected by the Acting Governor, the Hon. J. D. Rankine, as the person best able to command a majority in the House. But the coalition was an uneasy one and did not last for more than a year. The secession of three parliamentary members from the Congress Party to the Labour Party enabled Adams to gain full control of the government and, with his election victories in 1948, 1951 and 1956, his Party was to remain in power until its defeat at the polls in December, 1961.

Social Changes

It may be said that the first social revolution in the island was brought about when large-scale sugar production, based on African labour, took the place of a peasant economy, based on white indentured servants. The second revolution took place during the years following emancipation. And in 1937 it appeared that a third far-reaching revolution was to be the direct result of the impact of the modern working class movement on Barbados.

We have seen how the progressive movement broke the political power which the planters and the merchants had wielded in the island from time immemorial. It also built up an almost unique trade union movement. The most important task facing the island after 1937, if it was to follow a progressive yet stable policy, was to bring capital and labour together in a spirit of goodwill and harmony. Since most employers in business houses and plantations were white and the mass of the working population mixed or black, it seemed the easiest thing for the demagogue to appeal to the passions of the hour and to widen the differences between capital and labour.

It is to the credit of the Barbadians that right from the outset they saw the paramount importance of keeping the island on a steady keel by promoting the cause of conciliation. The progressive movement established the Barbados Workers Union as an organisation which functioned as a single union, with as many divisions as were necessary to cover the various trades and occupations in the island. In this way Barbados averted the situation in which numerous unions, springing up from various sides, could have given rise to industrial unrest and instability. This role the Barbados Workers Union played under the leadership of Grantley Adams and Hugh Springer. And there can be no doubt that, after the split in the joint leadership of the union and the political movement in 1954, the B.W.U. continued to exercise a progressive yet stabilising influence under the leadership of Frank Walcott.

The political triumphs of the Barbados Labour Party had to be followed by substantial benefits for the people of the island. An impressive volume of labour and social legislation was enacted to remedy some of the most glaring defects in the life of the community. Education, old age pensions and workmen's compensation, housing schemes, recreation facilities and cultural amenities, nutrition clinics and nurseries, health centres in St. Michael, St. Peter and St. Philip — these are only some of the many matters that called for the constant attention of the Progressives now that they were in power.

Economic Recovery
The people of the island realised that, whatever resounding triumphs were won in the political field, the bottom would still drop out of their world if the price of their staple product fell too low. Britain had increased the preference on sugar and international control had helped to bring about a small increase in its price. Yet the situation was far from being satisfactory. When the

Second World War came in 1939, there was no boom in sugar prices as there had been during 1914–18. Instead, the United Kingdom bought all our sugar at less than world market prices. This was a heavy disappointment to the planters of the island but they accepted it as an inevitable war-time burden.

When the war was over, Barbados and the other colonies of the West Indies hoped that the Mother Country would adopt a more generous policy. But they were sadly disappointed when the U.K. decided in 1948 to buy colonial sugar on the basis of 'world-market prices and other factors'. There was no offer of a long term agreement or of a price that would make up for the lean years of the war. Under such a policy, the West Indian territories dependent on agriculture seemed to have no prospect of attaining anything like a stable economy.

The planters of the area, led by R. L. Kirkwood of Jamaica, Sir Harold Robinson of Trinidad and Sir Archibald Cuke of Barbados, immediately took up the issue. They were supported by the political leaders of the West Indies and thus they succeeded in presenting a united national front. Eventually, after much negotiation, the Commonwealth Sugar Agreement was signed in 1951 and from this contract has come the comparative prosperity of Barbados in modern times.

The one disturbing feature is that the prosperity of our sugar depends on the generosity of the United Kingdom and that, without a long term agreement and a guaranteed price, Barbados could once again fall upon evil days. The Barbadians have therefore taken active measures to encourage other industries. In the first chapter we saw the success of these measures, especially in tourism, which is being rapidly developed as one of the main industries after sugar.

In this way, Barbados has been able to advance nearer and nearer to a position of stability. Not the least of the factors that led to this happy state of affairs were the good rainfall during the period 1949–1957 and the unusually large crops produced by the island. But, above all, Barbados has to be grateful that once again, as in every crisis in our history, we found the men who could rally support for a policy of wisdom and moderation and lead the island to a prosperous and stable position. Under such leadership the island appears to be making its way through the great social revolution of modern times without unduly disturbing any of the sections that make up our little community. Thus it would seem that the whole island is working together to maintain the long tradition of parliamentary government and to ensure that political democracy is a safeguard rather than a threat to its economic stability.

Further Reading

Story of the Progressive Movement by F. A. Hoyos.
Labour in the West Indies by Arthur Lewis.
The British West Indies — the Search for Self-Government by Morley Ayearst.
The Rise of West Indian Democracy by F. A. Hoyos.

Chapter 19

OUR SYSTEM OF GOVERNMENT

IN 1629, two years after the English settlers arrived in Barbados, the island was divided into six parishes. Then in 1645 the system was revised and eleven parishes were established in the island. These are still known to-day as St. Michael, Christ Church, St. James, St. Thomas, St. Philip, St. George, St. John, St. Joseph, St. Peter, St. Andrew and St. Lucy. In the map provided opposite this page you will see in what parts of the island these parishes are situated.

From earliest times until 1959, each of the parishes was governed by a Vestry. In St. Michael the Chairman of the Vestry was the Dean of the Cathedral and in the other Vestries the Rector of the parish was Chairman. The other members of the Vestry were elected at the beginning of each year. Their task was to care for the poor, to look after roads and to see that the Anglican churches were repaired and maintained in a good condition. To do all this the Vestry was empowered to raise money by levying rates every year on owners of property and on persons carrying on business in the parish.

The Vestries of the Church of England thus formed the island's system of local government, and it is appropriate here to follow the history of the Church in Barbados up to recent years, which have seen its disestablishment and the ending of its control of local government.

Sketch Map showing the Parishes of Barbados

The Anglican faith came to Barbados with the first settlement of the island. Churches were built and dedicated in accordance with English practice, the Anglican doctrine and discipline were declared to be binding both on clergy and laity, and the Book of Common Prayer was established as the standard of worship. Clergymen were appointed to livings by the Vestries who were responsible for their stipends. Later, they received their emoluments from the Public Treasury and the Governor exercised his prerogative as 'Ordinary of the Island' to make appointments to benefices. These arrangements were all instituted by Acts of the Legislature from time to time.

Unfortunately, it was decided right from the outset that the Christian Gospel should not be preached to the slaves. In spite of the protests of some of the clergy and the notable example of the Codrington Experiment, this policy was firmly maintained and the doors of the Established Church were closed to the African slaves for nearly two centuries. But with the appointment in 1825 of William Hart Coleridge as the first Bishop of Barbados a new epoch began in the life of the Church, as we have seen in Chapter 14. Thanks to his labours and to those who followed him, the Church of England ceased to be the Church of a minority of the population. By its work in education and in the pastoral field, added to the fact that it was the State Church, it won the allegiance of a majority of the people.

In 1870 the Colonial Office pressed for the passing of an Act to disestablish and disendow the Church of England but the feeling against the proposed legislation was so strong that it was abandoned. By 1871 89 per cent of the island's population were members of the Anglican Church. But the present century has seen a decline from 77 per cent in 1911 to 58 per cent in 1960.

It was probably due to its decline in numbers and influence that a campaign was launched in the 1920's to disestablish and disendow the Church of England. This time the inspiration came not from the Colonial Office but from the Democratic League led by O'Neale. With the growth of other Christian denominations, there was increasing support for the principle of religious equality. It was inevitable that the changing tide of opinion would influence the policy of the island's major parties. After the general elections of 1956 the first active steps were taken to disestablish and disendow the Church of England and the process was completed on March 31st, 1969. Thus the far-reaching measure first suggested by the Colonial Office and advocated by the Democratic League was later initiated by the Barbados Labour Party and brought to its logical conclusion by the Democratic Labour Party.

Local Government Changes
Early in 1959 a change was adopted in our system of local government. The island was divided into three areas which were known as the city of Bridgetown, the Southern District and the Northern District. Bridgetown became a municipal city with a Mayor and City Council to administer its affairs. The two other areas were governed by two Councils known as the Northern District Council and the Southern District Council. The three Councils in charge of these districts took over the services formerly rendered by the eleven Vestries.

One of the changes introduced by the new system of local government should be specially mentioned here. The Councils did not, like the old Vestries, play any part in the running of Church affairs. The Rector of a parish was no longer the chairman of any local authority and no

member of the Councils was expected to function as a
member of a Church committee. In the past the Vestries
used to repair Church properties and pay the salaries of a
number of Church officers, but the Councils handed over
such responsibilities to the various religious bodies to
whom they made annual grants for the purpose.

Other important changes were brought in by the
new system. The old Vestries were elected on a narrow
franchise which gave the vote to only a small portion of the
island's population. The new Councils were elected under
adult suffrage — in other words, every one over the age
of twenty-one years was allowed to vote. The life of the
Vestry lasted for one year only, but that of the Councils
extended over a period of three years. Under the old
order, there was a complicated system of local taxation,
but the aim of the new system was to establish a more
uniform system of Rating and Trade Tax. Moreover,
whereas the Central Government had no clear control
over the Vestries in financial matters, the former super-
vised the income and expenditure of the local government
authorities.

A Short Term

The Vestries had lasted for three centuries but the
Councils that took their place, on the advice of a specialist
in the field, Sir John Maude, did not survive a decade.

In 1964, Dr. Richard Jackson was appointed to consider the reorganisation of local government services.
Two years later, it was decided to transfer Public Health

Inspectors from the Local Government Councils to the Central Government. These new Councils were dissolved in 1967 and the functions that had been performed by them were transferred to an Interim Commissioner for Local Government, who was made responsible for the over-all running of the services previously administered by the Councils and Aldermen.

On August 31, 1969, the Interim Commissioner was relieved of his duties. Responsibility for the various services concerned was assigned to the Central Government. For example, Infirmaries, now called District Hospitals, were placed under the supervision of the Ministry of Health. Rating and Taxation were placed under the control of the Ministry of Finance.

In addition, statutory boards were created to take over other functions previously performed by the Councils. These boards have their constitutions, functions and procedure laid down in the statute law of the island and their members are appointed by the appropriate Minister. They are responsible for the management of certain departments not directly under the control of the Government, though the latter maintains its influence through the members it appoints for a limited period and through the power it enjoys of revoking the appointment of any of these members.

There has been a gradual expansion of the island's health services. District Hospitals and out-patient clinics have been established in outlying areas in order to relieve the pressure on the Queen Elizabeth Hospital. Among the statutory boards recently appointed is one which goes under the curious name of Sanitation and Cemeteries Board. It sees that general health regulations are carried out, keeps a vigilant watch on the proper disposal of garbage and on the dangers of over-crowding, and ensures that the cemeteries are kept in good condition.

Day nurseries and children's homes have become the responsibility of the Child Care Board. At the day nurseries, working mothers can leave their children in pleasant surroundings from early morning till late in the evening. The Government also gives financial assistance

The Queen Elizabeth Hospital

to day nurseries run by voluntary organisations, provided they conform to certain standards. Children's homes provide residences for homeless children. People are encouraged to visit these homes, to make the acquaintance of the children and to take them out as frequently as possible. In this way, it is hoped that an increasing number of persons will eventually adopt these children.

Old Age Pensions, which are now administered by the Chief Welfare Officer in an expanded Social Welfare Department, provide $20.00 a week for men and women who are sixty-five years old or more. While Old Age Pensions are given on a permanent basis, National Assistance grants are only temporary and are given to people in need to help tide them over a difficult period until they can find work. Educational Assistance provides children in need either with money to buy books and lunch or with assistance in kind, such as clothing and school uniforms.

In addition to these non-contributory services there is also the National Insurance Scheme, one of the most ambitious projects in recent times, under which citizens become eligible for pensions and for sickness and other benefits, in return for regular payments.

All the services that were once administered by the Councils have now been transferred to the Central Government or to statutory boards under the control of the Central Government. Events have followed one another with almost astonishing rapidity. The new system of local government was established in 1959. The Councils were abolished in 1967 and the entire new organisation for running district services was finally dissolved when the post of Interim Commissioner for Local Government was terminated at the end of August, 1969.

A Long Tradition

The legislature of Barbados goes even farther back in history than our original system of local government. The island was settled on February 17, 1627, and in less than four months it was guaranteed free political institutions by Charles I, who was then the King of England. But the Royal Charter making this grant was not carried into effect immediately. Still, the legislature of this island has an ancient history, of which we should be quite proud, and I want to tell you something of its origin before we go any further.

The office of Governor goes right back to the beginning of the settlement. He appointed a number of men to advise him and they formed his Council. Later the Governor's Council came to be known as the Legislative Council.

As you read in Chapter 8, the House of Assembly was established in 1639. This makes it, after the British Parliament and Bermuda House of Assembly, the oldest legislative body in the Commonwealth. In 1652 the Articles of Agreement signed by Barbados and the Government of Oliver Cromwell confirmed that the government of this island should consist of a Governor, Council and Assembly.

To-day the structure of Government in Barbados remains basically the same as it has been for many years. The House of Assembly is now made up of 24 members, one from each of the 24 constituencies which were created in 1971. The Second Chamber, previously the legislative Council, exists to-day as the Senate, which has 21 members, 12 of whom are selected by the party in power, two by the Opposition and seven by the Governor-General. The duties of the Secretary of State in appointing public officers have been taken over by the various Service Commissions — the Public Service Commission, the Legal and Judicial Service Commission and the Police Service Commission.

The House of Assembly in Session

These appointments are confirmed by the Governor-General.

Important Changes

Although our system of government remains in many respects the same, there have been a number of important changes through the years. In 1831, for instance, the free coloured people were given the right to vote for members of the House of Assembly. After the abolition of slavery, the emancipated classes were not debarred from the franchise, though the qualifications for voting were made very high. The number of electors then registered to vote was 1,641.

Another advance was made in 1884 when the freehold qualification was lowered to £5 and an income qualification of £50 per annum was introduced. The first result of this was to increase the number of voters to 2,004. In 1944 the income qualification was reduced from £50 to £20 per annum. This had the effect of enfranchising thousands of artisans and agricultural labourers and their womenfolk, who were given the vote for the first time. This process reached its logical conclusion when adult franchise was introduced in 1951 and in 1963 the franchise was further extended, this time to all males and females who were eighteen years old or more. With these changes, the number of registered voters now stands at approximately 110,000.

You will see, therefore, how the basis of the island's system of government was gradually widened. With the passing of time, more and more people were admitted to the duties and privileges of citizenship until the point was reached where every adult, whether male or female, was given the opportunity to select the members of the House of Assembly.

Now we must give our attention to other changes in the island's constitution. You will then see how naturally and logically the cause of democracy was advanced in the island. First the mass of the people were given the right to vote and now you will learn how the members they selected for the Assembly were given more and more control of the island's government.

In 1881, the Executive Committee was established as the chief instrument of government policy. This consisted of the Governor, who presided over its meetings, his official advisers, four members of the House of Assembly, and one member of the Legislative Council. For the first time in the island's history, members of the Assembly were thus given the opportunity to advise on official policy. This system worked well for quite a number of years, with the Attorney General in charge of government business in the Assembly.

The Sovereign Power

In 1946, a change of no little significance took place when the person best able to command a majority in the Assembly was asked, under the Bushe Experiment, to suggest the names of the four members of the Assembly who should be members of the Executive Committee. This was a step in the direction of responsible government under which the elected representatives of the people become responsible for the administration of the island's affairs.

This process was taken yet another stage further when a Ministerial system of government was introduced in February 1954. Under this system, five Ministers assumed responsibility for certain departments of government. One of the significant things in this system was that the leader of the government party in the Assembly was given the title of Premier.

The next stage in this business of transferring power to the elected representatives of the people was, with the approval of the Legislature, to set up a cabinet system of government in Barbados. Under this system, the Cabinet took the place of the Executive Committee as

The Government Headquarters, or 'Ministerial Building'

the chief instrument of policy. The Premier presided over meetings of the Cabinet and the Governor as the Queen's representative assumed the role of a constitutional monarch.

In due course, the island's constitution was advanced a stage further. Barbados was granted complete internal self-government and later, as we shall see, proceeded to complete independence. The Governor of the island became Governor-General and the Premier became Prime Minister. The first Governor-General was Sir John Stow, who was succeeded by Sir Winston Scott. The latter was the first native Governor-General of the island and Errol Barrow, of whom you will read more in a later chapter, was the first Prime Minister.

The changes we have mentioned above show one very important development. The House of Assembly, following the example of the House of Commons, has gradually established itself as the sovereign power of the land. No public money can be spent without its approval and, by controlling the Prime Minister and the Cabinet, it controls the administration of the island's government.

The Judicial System

A brief explanation has been given of the island's Legislature and of the changes and subsequent abolition of our system of local government. But no form of government can be effective unless the laws are observed and justice administered. That is why the island's judicial system is so important.

Barbados is divided into five magisterial districts, and Magistrates preside over courts in each district for the purpose of hearing civil and criminal cases. The densely populated parish of St. Michael and part of the parish of Christ Church are known as District A, and several Magistrates are required to look after the many cases that come before this court. District B consists of the parish of St. George and most of the parish of Christ Church, District C of St. Philip and St. John, District D of St. Thomas, District E of St. James, St. Peter and St. Lucy and District F of St. Joseph and St. Andrew.

After changes made in 1956, appeals from the Magistrates' courts could be made to the divisional court of the Supreme Court, over which two judges preside. With the advent of independence, Barbados established its own Court of Appeal and appeals from Magistrates' Courts now go to a Divisional Court of two judges from whom appeals, on points of law only, lie to the Court of Appeal. Her Majesty's Judicial Committee of the Privy Council in London remains the final Court of Appeal in all matters.

The law which applies in Barbados is by and large the common law of England. The common law of Barbados, however, is taken to be the common law of England along with the statutes of England in existence prior to the date of the settlement in 1627. In addition, the courts administer the statute laws of Barbados which consist of acts, rules and regulations passed by the island's Parliament.

In the old days when there was a Grand Jury and the Chief Justice addressed them in what was called a Charge, the opening of the Assizes in March, July and November was an impressive occasion. Gradually a great deal of this ceremony has been abandoned. Yet there is still much to impress the spectator to-day when the Criminal Division of the Supreme Court opens its assizes. The fanfare of trumpets by the heralds, the robes of the Chief Justice and his brother judges, the smart uniforms of the police-men, combine to give an idea of the majesty of the law.

But even more important than this appearance of majesty is the confidence which Barbadians have always had in the island's administration of justice. They are convinced that all men, irrespective of race or colour, will be fairly tried. And they take no little pride in the fact that Barbadians have held the highest positions in the judicial service and discharged their responsible duties with honour to themselves and to the island. So high is the esteem in which our Judges are held that the Chief Justice of Barbados, Sir William Douglas, has recently been appointed a member of Her Majesty's Judicial Committee of the Privy Council.

Further Reading

Report on Local Government in Barbados
     by Sir John Maude, K.C.B., K.B.E., 1949.
Report on Local Government in Barbados by Dr. Richard Jackson.
Ten Years of Constitutional Development in Barbados
     by J. M. Hewitt.
Road to Responsible Government by F. A. Hoyos.

Chapter 20

EDUCATING OUR PEOPLE

BY now you have read quite enough of the great triumphs which the Barbadians have usually won over the most adverse circumstances in their history. We may safely say that those triumphs were achieved largely because the people of this island always attached the greatest importance to education. It is fitting, therefore, to pause here for a moment and consider the work which has been done in the past to advance the cause of education, and the institutions which have been established through the wisdom and foresight of our ancestors.

During the early years after the settlement of the island, the planters and merchants who had the wherewithal sent their children to England to be educated. Those who could not afford to do this sent their children to the few private schools which existed in Barbados at that time. No one seemed to care very much whether the children of the 'poor whites' received any education at all. And certainly nothing was done, except on the Codrington estates at a later date, to instruct the Negro slaves even in the elements of the Christian religion.

In 1686 the first attempt was made to educate the children of the underprivileged. We should honour the names of two planters, John Elliott and Rowland Bulkeley of the parish of St. George, because they set up the first school for the children of the 'poor whites'. Although it was limited to the children of one race, this 'charity school', as it was called, was the first step in the campaign to bring the benefits of education to the children of the underprivileged.

Other wealthy planters who helped to establish charity schools for poor white children were Henry Drax, who left a substantial sum of money for the building of a school in Bridgetown, and Francis Williams, who gave a hundred acres of land for a similar institution in Christ Church. Out of these two bequests came the schools that were later to be known as Combermere School and the Boys' Foundation School.

One of the most far-reaching steps in the early eighteenth century was the foundation of Harrison's Free School by Thomas Harrison, the Churchwarden of St. Michael. It was established with the same purpose as other charity schools in the island but it was destined to have a distinguished history. For it became the Harrison College of modern times, a school with a scholastic and athletic record surpassed by no other school in the West Indies.

You will remember that I told you about Christopher Codrington in an earlier chapter. One result of his bequest was that the Codrington Grammar School was opened in 1745 with the primary purpose of educating boys who could consequently be trained for Holy Orders. That later came to be known as the Lodge School and to-day it is recognised as one of the leading schools in the South Caribbean.

Preparing for Freedom

During all this time nothing was done to provide education for the children of the Negroes. But as the nineteenth century began its course, Barbados realised that slavery was doomed and that something should be done to prepare the slaves for the day of freedom. Nothing could be better, it was felt, than to equip the coloured people through education for the privileges and responsibilities that lay ahead of them in the future.

When you pass through Mason Hall Street in the city of Bridgetown, you will see a building looking something like a Masonic Temple and housing the St. Mary's Elementary School. It is a landmark in the history of

Codrington College

Barbadian education and you should show it some mark
of respect and honour. For it was the first elementary
school established in this island for coloured boys. The
original building, which is no longer in existence, was
paid for by public subscription and the Church Missionary Society helped with its running expenses.

That was in 1818 and the following year Combermere
School, which was first a charity school for poor white
children, was reorganised and a number of coloured
children admitted to its classes. When Bishop Coleridge
came to Barbados in 1825, he was so impressed with these
developments in Barbadian education that he worked with
might and main to encourage the liberal trend in the
island's education policy. Largely through his efforts, the
first elementary school for coloured girls was established
in 1827 and after that the facilities for primary education,
so sadly neglected in the past, were rapidly developed to
meet the crisis of those times. For Coleridge and the
far-sighted patriots who helped him realised that the
children of the slaves must be educated to meet the
challenge of a changing era.

The Mitchinson Commission

But the great improvements that produced our modern
educational system were yet to come. For these improvements we have to thank Bishop Mitchinson, who was the
Chairman of the 1875 Education Commission, which
urged the Government to give more active support to the
work of educating the island's children. As a result of

that Commission's report, three First Grade Secondary Schools were established under government auspices, Harrison College and The Lodge School for boys and Queen's College for girls. One of the main objects of these schools was to prepare boys and girls for entry to the universities and it is fortunate for Barbados that these schools succeeded in building up a sound academic reputation.

The Mitchinson Commission also inspired the establishment of a number of Second Grade Schools to provide instruction intermediate between the primary schools and the First Grade Schools. The first of the Second Grade Schools to be set up was Combermere School, which was reorganised for the purpose in 1879. Two years later followed the Coleridge School in St. Peter, the Alleyne School in St. Andrew and the Parry School in St. Lucy. Then came the Alexandra School in St. Peter and the Foundation School in Christ Church, which were duly recognised as Second Grade Schools. To complete the picture we should mention here that the St. Michael's Girls' School was established in 1928 and that Coleridge and Parry Schools were combined and made into one Second Grade School in 1952.

The Mitchinson Commission did not confine itself to the question of secondary education. As a result of its recommendations Barbados set up a network of primary schools and established exhibitions that helped many of the poorest children to receive the best education the island had to offer. Since the Barbados Scholarship, thanks mainly to Bishop Mitchinson, was established in 1879, the island could now boast that the poorest of its underprivileged children, if they had outstanding ability, could proceed to the learned professions with the help of the state.

Moreover, Codrington College was affiliated to the University of Durham in 1875, again through the exertions of Bishop Mitchinson, and students could now be trained not only for the Ministry but for degrees in Classics after which they could go on to one or other of the professions. From that date until the opening of the University College of the West Indies in Jamaica in 1947, Barbados enjoyed a unique reputation, for it was the only territory where education was provided in all its stages from the primary school to the university level. Thanks to the work of Codrington College, Barbadians were trained to fill prominent positions both in the Church and in the field of education in most of the neighbouring West Indian territories.

Expanding the System

Pleased though it was with its achievements. Barbados was not satisfied to rest on its laurels. In 1912 a training college was established for male teachers and three years later similar facilities were provided for women teachers. The Rawle Training Institute, as it was called, was a West Indian institution drawing its students from the Windward and Leeward Islands as well as from Guyana. More recently, the facilities for training teachers were greatly expanded by the establishment of Erdiston Training College which was opened in 1948.

Barbados took a step in keeping with modern trends when it made instruction in its 124 primary schools free. Besides bringing teaching methods up to date, subjects were added to the curriculum so as to relate it more closely to the environment of the pupils. But the twentieth century saw a vastly increased demand for secondary education. Private schools like the Ursuline Convent and the Codrington High School were established to meet a part of this demand. Other independent schools were also started and a number of these were later approved by the Ministry of Education as fit to take certain public examinations. The Ministry itself undertook to meet some of the demand by providing secondary education in the senior classes of the primary schools. And not the least of its contributions was to make education at the Government Secondary Schools free.

All of these efforts, however, were far from adequate to satisfy the clamour for secondary education and quite recently Barbados therefore started on the important venture of establishing secondary modern schools. Barbadian educators were convinced that the great improvements of the nineteenth century had provided benefits only for a section of the island's population, and that, if secondary education was to be given to all, our system would have to be expanded and diversified.

That is the vitally important purpose of the secondary modern schools which aim at reaching all the children of the island by teaching a syllabus that will develop their aptitudes and skills. At the present time there are seven secondary modern schools in the island and Barbadians hope that men and women of outstanding ability will be found to develop an increasing number of these schools and bring them to the highest possible level of achievement and prestige. In keeping with the policy of democratising education in the island, all schools providing secondary education, whether First Grade, Second Grade, Secondary Modern or Comprehensive, have come to be known simply as secondary schools.

Meeting Other Requirements
Attention has also been given to other requirements in the field of education. The Barbados Community College has been established to extend and diversify the facilities for sixth form education in the island. Classes have been provided in Liberal Arts, Science and Commerce and others will be added in Agriculture and Fine Arts. A Division of Technology will provide training for technicians.

Perhaps the most significant enterprise in recent years has been the establishment of a Polytechnic, appropriately named after one of the greatest Barbadians of all time. The aims of Samuel Jackman Prescod Polytechnic are to develop trades and skills, to meet the requirements of the labour market for skilled operatives and craftsmen, to prepare students for direct entry into paid employment or for entry into the Division of Technology of the Barbados Community College.

The Princess Margaret Secondary Modern School: the Pride of
India tree on the left was planted by H.R.H. Princess Margaret.

To integrate the Polytechnic in the island's educational system, a number of changes and adjustments
have been made. The most important decision was to
close the Technical Institute, the functions of which were
to be assured by the Polytechnic. It was also decided to
transfer certain courses to the Polytechnic from the
Barbados Evening Institute, which would however still
serve the island with courses not provided in the programmes of other institutions. The Extra-Mural Department of the University of the West Indies, too, continues
to make its contribution by arranging classes and lectures
and organising youth groups in some of our rural areas.

Barbados has every reason to be proud of the educational institutions it has built up over the years. These institutions were established on sound principles and have produced results that have long placed the island in the van of West Indian education. Yet, with the changing ideas of the twentieth century, it was essential to modernise our educational system and that is the task to which Barbados is presently devoting its efforts. Now, more than ever before, we are committed to the great enterprise of educating our people.

The Cave Hill Campus

When the University College of the West Indies was established at Mona, Jamaica, in 1947, Barbados gave its whole-hearted support and co-operation to the venture. Since then a regional and autonomous university has arisen, with its centre at Mona, with Faculties of Engineering and Agriculture in St. Augustine, Trinidad, and with a College of Arts and Science in Barbados which is now Cave Hill Campus.

Teaching began at the College in October 1963 and four years later it was moved to its permanent site at Cave Hill. The development of the Cave Hill Campus has been made possible by munificent grants from Britain and Canada, with France also helping by supplying lecturers in French under assistance schemes.

The contributions of the Government and people of Barbados have been the site at Cave Hill, and the access road, extending over an area of forty-six acres. Free

University of the West Indies Cave Hill Campus

tuition was provided at the College for all of the Barbadian students. In addition, Barbados increased its contribution to the regional university by giving more than one million dollars annually in the period from 1967 to 1969.

A substantial portion of the British grant was made on the condition that the Cave Hill Campus would be developed in such a manner and to such an extent as to attract students from the Leeward and Windward Islands. This condition was readily accepted and plans were prepared and have already been largely implemented to make appropriate courses available and to secure provision for scholarships, bursaries and maintenance allowances.

In all this, Barbados demonstrated its earnest desire to make the Cave Hill Campus an integral part of the University of the West Indies and to provide facilities and courses for students from the Leeward and Windward group as well as from Belize and the British Virgin Islands and The Bahamas.

A considerable number of organisations, business firms and private individuals also contributed generously not only to the development of the Cave Hill Campus generally but for the provision of facilities for students' amenities and activities.

In April 1968, the Centre for Multiracial Studies was established on two acres of land adjoining the Cave Hill Campus and given by the Barbados Government for the purpose. The Centre functioned in close association with the University of the West Indies and Sussex University, and was dedicated to the study, at graduate level, of multiracial societies. Unfortunately, the centre is now closed but its library is administered by staff of the Cave Hill Campus and its facilities are still available to the serious student.

At the laying of the foundation stone of the Cave Hill Campus, one of the speakers ventured the prophecy that in time a new city would arise around the new institution. The College would be surrounded by all the artifacts of a modern community and there would be thousands of homes, primary and secondary schools, churches, theatres, cinemas, shopping centres and recreation grounds, highways and shaded walks. It is a dream that might well be realised, a prophecy that might well be fulfilled, before many years have passed into history.

Further Reading

Report of the Mitchinson Commission on Education (1875).
Proposals for the Establishment of the Samuel Jackman Prescod Polytechnic.
Bishop Rawle — A Memoir by G. Mather and C. J. Blagg.
A Century of West Indian Education by Shirley G. Gordon.

Chapter 21

BARBADOS AND FEDERATION

THE history of Barbados had shown that Barbadians at all levels had many things in common, that had gradually brought them together over the years. Their experiences in the past had given them a sense of oneness. Their trials and suffering and triumphs had convinced them that, in spite of differences of race and colour, they formed a single community that was as closely knit as any other plural society in the world.

But there were certain trends in the West Indies which Barbados could not ignore and to which she had to adjust herself. These trends could be clearly seen in a number of events and developments in the area. There were institutions like the Imperial College of Tropical Agriculture, established in Trinidad in 1924, and the Sugar Cane Breeding Station, set up in Barbados in 1931, which were designed to meet more than merely insular needs. There were the declarations of the Dominica Conference in 1932 and the Caribbean Labour Conference in 1938 that came out strongly in favour of West Indian federation. There was West Indian cricket that was doing its share to bring the people of the various territories together as West Indians. There was the University of the West Indies already serving as a focus of West Indian activities and as the rallying centre of West Indian life and thought.

The Achievement of Bim

Along with all these trends was a powerful cultural up-
surge manifesting itself in prose and poetry, in painting
and sculpture. It is here that we must make some mention of the contribution of *Bim* magazine to the literary
and artistic movement of the area. Started in 1942, its
earliest editors were Jimmy Cozier, Hal Evelyn, Therold
Barnes and Frank Collymore. As some of these dropped
out, their places were taken by others such as Edward
Brathwaite, John Wickham and Freddie Forde.

Insular in its scope at the beginning, *Bim* soon began
to widen its horizon and adapt itself to the changing West
Indian scene. Instinctively, and perhaps almost uncon-
sciously, it played a significant part in the development of
West Indian thought and West Indian awareness. Its
policy was simply to encourage creative writing in the
area. It published short stories, poems, critical articles and
reviews. It sought to encourage all those who wanted to
write and it is a remarkable fact that so many West Indian
writers who later won recognition at home and abroad
began their career by contributing to *Bim*. Those who
were first encouraged by *Bim* to express themselves in
prose and poetry are to-day among the major figures of
West Indian literature — Edgar Mittelholzer of Guyana,
Samuel Selvon of Trinidad, Derek Walcott of St. Lucia,
Edward Brathwaite and George Lamming of Barbados.

To-day Derek Walcott and Edward Brathwaite are
regarded as two of the leading poets in the area. Edgar
Mittelholzer was, right to the end, the most prolific of all

West Indian writers. Samuel Selvon has won wide fame by his humour and the accurate portrayal of his fellow West Indians. And George Lamming, essentially a poet, has produced novels that are really prose poems which have earned him international renown.

There are many others who are grateful to *Bim* for giving them a medium through which they could reach a sensitive reading public. Austin Clarke, Timothy Callendar and John Wickham, John Figueroa, Mervyn Morris and Geoffrey Drayton, Gloria Escoffery, Monica Skeete and A. J. Seymour — the list could go on almost indefinitely.

The man who was mainly, if not almost entirely, responsible for the continued existence of *Bim* was Frank Collymore. As editor, publisher and business manager, he worked with unremitting energy and enthusiasm to inspire and encourage the writers of the West Indies. It was a fitting recognition of his work when the University of the West Indies conferred on him the degree of M.A., *honoris causa*, recording in the citation that through *Bim* he had 'done more than any other single individual to foster the recent growth and flowering of West Indian literature'.

A New Adventure

The creative activity I have just referred to was only one aspect of the general awakening that had occurred throughout the West Indies. Barbados, like other neighbouring territories, was caught up in the new spirit that was abroad in the area. It felt itself to be part of a West Indian community that was moving towards the ideal of West Indian unity and co-operation.

Thus it was in 1958 Barbados entered upon a new adventure. It became a member of the Federation of the West Indies and set out on the experiment to link the islands of the British West Indies more closely together. It joined the Federation, of its own free will, for one of the most important reasons. It felt that just as Barbados, with its varying sections, had certain common interests and certain common ambitions, so the West Indies, in spite of their different peoples, had a sufficiently large number of things in common to make the British Caribbean a single community.

This sense of a West Indian community is a fairly recent thing. In 1876, you will remember, Barbados defeated the Colonial Office plan for federation because it did not want to lose its system of self-government. Barbados considered that it was far more important to keep its free institutions than to support a federal plan based on the Crown Colony system. And as recently as 1921 a Royal Commission reported that there was so much insularity in the West Indies — each island was so selfishly interested only in its own welfare — that federation would be difficult if not impossible.

The Democratic Movement

It was the democratic movement after the first world war that changed the ideas of the people of the West Indies.

Its leaders launched a campaign of political education aimed at teaching the people to think along national rather than insular lines. The outstanding men of the movement were Cipriani of Trinidad, Marryshow of Grenada and Rawle of Dominica. Slowly but surely these three men and their followers succeeded in spreading the idea that the islands of the West Indies must be united if they were to succeed in surviving amid the many complexities of the modern world.

The unquestioned leader of this campaign was Cipriani. His opinion on West Indian Federation was as clear-cut as that of the Barbadian patriots of 1876, but it was inspired by a more thorough-going democratic spirit. You may have heard your parents speak of his famous slogan, 'No Federation without Self-government, No Self-government without Adult Suffrage'. In other words, Cipriani wanted the West Indies to be united and self-governing with all the people playing their part in the business of government.

Gradually, Cipriani's ideas were accepted throughout the West Indies. Barbados, which earlier had herself retained the right of self-government, watched with sympathy the struggle to overthrow the Crown Colony system and establish a federation based on free institutions. When each of the islands was given more control of its own affairs, Cipriani's movement, which continued to gather momentum after his death in 1945, became even more successful. And when it became clear that federation would not stand in the way of the political progress of the individual islands, Barbados showed her willingness to accept a plan for closer association.

Barbados was represented at the Montego Bay Conference in 1947 and at every federation parley after that by two of her elder statesmen, Sir Grantley Adams and Sir Archibald Cuke. These two men brought the benefit of their experience and ability to all the negotiations that were necessary and they attended the Conference in London when federation was finally accepted in February 1956. By 1958 Barbados had none of the fears she entertained in 1876. Although she, along with Jamaica, had recently attained the honour of Cabinet Government, she remained serenely confident that joining the Federation

The Montego Bay Conference, 1947: the delegates in session

would mean no constitutional set-back for her, as it might have done in 1876.

You will recall that a Fact-Finding Commission sent out by the British Government recommended that Barbados should be the site of the capital of the new Federation. It was a great honour for us. It was naturally pleasing to Barbadians because it recognised that the island, with its geographical position, its climate, its educational institutions, its long tradition of parliamentary government and its atmosphere of political and industrial stability, was best suited to be the home of the Federal capital. But the Standing Federation Committee, at their meeting in Jamaica in 1957, rejected the Commission's recommendation and decided to place the Federal capital not in Barbados, but in Trinidad.

That decision was loyally and cheerfully accepted by the Barbadians, for they realised that the really important thing was not which island won the coveted prize of the capital but that the Federation should be a success. Moreover, they were well aware that, wherever the capital was sited, they would still be able to bring their long experience of self-government to bear on the task of making the Federation a success. It was, perhaps, not without significance that a Barbadian, Sir Grantley Adams, was elected as the first Federal Prime Minister and another Barbadian, E. R. L. Ward, was chosen by the Federal House of Representatives as their Speaker. A Barbadian by adoption, Dr. A. S. (later Sir Arnott) Cato, was appointed President of the Federal Senate.

The Case for Federation

No one questioned the benefits that Jamaica, Trinidad and Barbados could gain from the Federation. With their growing industrial enterprises, they would be stimulated to greater efforts by having the whole market of the British Caribbean to consume their goods; and Barbados, in particular, hoped to find an outlet for her surplus population in some of the neighbouring territories. Just as the poor people in the Island in 1876 wanted federation because Pope-Hennessy promised it would give them employment in the Windward Islands, so Barbados in 1958 hoped to find in the developing economy of the new West Indies ample scope for the efficient labour force she had always been able to supply in abundance.

But it was the general feeling that the value of the West Indian Federation should not be assessed by the benefit it could bring to any particular island. The importance of the federal experiment lay in what it could do for the area as a whole. Two main arguments were adduced in favour of West Indian Federation and their purpose was to make it clear that the demand for closer union and co-operation between the islands of the British Caribbean was based on certain hard realities.

In the first place, it was considered obvious that, by pooling their resources, the West Indies could produce better things and, by negotiating together, they could obtain better prices for what they produced. This had already been the case with such crops as sugar, bananas and citrus fruit. It was felt that the Federal Government would now do more thoroughly what the separate islands had hitherto tried to do by combining from time to time for certain purposes.

The second argument for West Indian Federation was equally important. The fact that Barbados governed itself explained why Barbadians enjoyed the priceless qualities of self-confidence and self-respect. If the West Indies showed they could govern themselves, they, too, would earn the respect of the world and of themselves. A West Indian nation, united and self-governing, developing its own resources and standing on its own feet, would be able to travel the shortest path towards independence for its people within the framework of the British Commonwealth.

In 1940 the Mother Country appointed a Comptroller for Development and Welfare in the West Indies and he was given a team of technical and research officers to help him in his task. For eighteen years Barbados had been the home of the Comptroller's Department and we had been able to see at first hand the efforts to develop the resources of the West Indies. This tremendous task was now taken over by the new Federal Government.

The situation facing the West Indies was very interesting. But it was by no means an easy one. The West Indian Federation was unique because its parts were separated by considerable stretches of sea water. Moreover, the West Indian community was composed not of one but of several different races and peoples. But these were factors that made the situation a challenge and an opportunity.

Barbadians had discovered from their own past that they invariably overcame their difficulties when they pulled together as a community. Would the West Indians, they asked, embark on the great adventure before them as a united group and would they attempt the tasks of the future not as scattered islands but as a single community dedicated to a common purpose?

As it turned out, the federal experiment was to prove a melancholy fiasco. Started with high hopes in April 1958, the Federation was ingloriously dissolved on May 31st, 1962. The reasons for this failure will provide the historians for many years with a fruitful subject for investigation and research. For the moment, we must confine ourselves to a few of the factors that contributed to that failure.

At an early stage, unhappy differences occurred within the ranks of the West Indies Federal Labour Party. Norman Manley, though he was President of the Party, declined to stand for election to the Federal Parliament. Not surprisingly, his People's National Party was defeated in the federal elections in Jamaica. Eric Williams made a similar decision and it is perhaps significant that his People's National Movement was also defeated in the federal elections in Trinidad. As a result, Grantley Adams, when he became Prime Minister, enjoyed only a slim majority in the Federal Parliament and this was one of the reasons why his Government was unable to take decisive action in times of crisis.

But personalities apart, it may perhaps be said that

there were two fundamental reasons why the federal experiment failed. First, there were the basic differences that arose between Jamaica and Trinidad on such vital issues as a Customs Union, Freedom of Movement and the powers of the Federal Government. Secondly, the Montego Bay Conference in 1947 made a tragic mistake when it failed to insist that West Indian Federation should, in the words of Roy Marshall, be the one and only means of securing political independence for the area as a whole.

In the event, Jamaica and Trinidad, when confronted with their sharply divergent views, considered themselves free to press for their individual independence. After a referendum on the issue in September 1961, Jamaica decided to secede from the Federation the following year. After this momentous decision, Williams made the grim mathematical jest that one from ten left zero. This clearly indicated that for him the federal union, without Jamaica as a member, was doomed to swift, inevitable extinction. Accordingly, in August 1962 Trinidad followed Jamaica's example and left the Federation.

Further Reading

The Federation of the West Indies: The End of an Experiment
    by Professor O. R. Marshall.
Federal Negotiations by Sir John Mordecai.
Reflections on the Failure of the First West Indian Federation
    by Hugh W. Springer.

Chapter 22

THE ROAD BACK

In December 1961, the Barbados Labour Party, led by Grantley Adams, was defeated at the polls by the Democratic Labour Party, under the leadership of Errol Barrow. At first sight, this would appear to suggest that the federal cause had been extinguished in the island and that Barbados had reverted to the insularity of former years. For in the election campaign the Barbados Labour Party appeared to be mainly pre-occupied with the case for West Indian Federation, while the Democratic Labour Party seemed to concentrate almost entirely on local issues.

But there is a danger in over-simplifying the situation and for this reason a number of factors and developments must be borne in mind.

After their abandonment by Jamaica and Trinidad and Tobago, the remaining territories of the Federation resolved to form a closer association among themselves. Errol Barrow's Government at once took up the challenge and gave its support to the federal cause represented by the Little Eight. But the disruptive influences that had destroyed the Federation of the Ten soon began to plague the efforts to establish a Federation of the Eight. It was a story that was now becoming painfully familiar to West Indians, with envy, confusion and disunity baulking the negotiations to get the Little Eight off the ground.

Independence Alone

By now, too, it was becoming clear, from past experience and present tribulations, that there were genuine difficulties in the way of regional co-operation. Such difficulties made protracted negotiations inevitable and this led to a certain degree of impatience in some quarters. As a result, the new Government of Barbados decided to opt for independence alone, thus following the example of Jamaica and Trinidad and Tobago. Barbados proceeded to independence as a separate territory on November 30th, 1966, and Errol Barrow, as we said in an earlier chapter, became the first Prime Minister of the island as an independent country.

This decision, however, did not go unquestioned. There was a great public debate before Barbados decided to go it alone and it is perhaps not without significance that a number of young men, calling themselves the Under Forties, waged a vigorous campaign, questioning the wisdom of opting for independence alone and urging that negotiations should be continued for independence within a Federation of the Little Eight.

Certainly, the concept of West Indian federation did not appear to be dead. Further evidence of this is shown by the attitudes of the two major parties on the issue. The Barbados Labour Party acquiesced in the inevitable and accepted the idea of Barbados as an independent island, but it never ceased to proclaim its allegiance to the cause of West Indian Federation. And the Democratic Labour Party took the first step in a renewed effort at

Tom Adams, Prime Minister,
1976–1985

Errol Barrow, Prime Minister,
1961–1976 and 1986–1987

Erskine Sandiford, Prime Minister

regional co-operation by agreeing to the proposal for a free trade area with Antigua, Guyana and Barbados as its first members. Moreover, there was general agreement when a provision was included in the new constitution of Barbados to the effect that the island could become closely associated with another territory in the West Indies by a simple majority decision of its legislature.

CARIFTA to CARICOM

Undoubtedly, the most important step on the road back to West Indian unity was the establishment of the Caribbean Free Trade Association. Work on the preamble of the Agreement instituting CARIFTA, as it was to be called, started in 1965. That preamble expressed the view that the territories concerned would share a common determination to satisfy the hopes and aspirations of their peoples for full employment and improved living conditions. Such an objective could best be attained by rapid economic development. West Indians could achieve such development only by broadening their domestic markets and eliminating trade barriers between the territories. And these barriers could be removed only by the establishment of a free trade area which would be gradually extended to include as many territories as possible in the Caribbean.

After much discussion, CARIFTA was established on May 1st, 1968. At first, it embraced Antigua, Barbados, Guyana and Trinidad and Tobago. In August of the same year, however, it was extended to include Jamaica and the Leeward and Windward Islands. Realising the limitations of Carifta, leaders in the Commonwealth Caribbean in 1974 signed the Treaty of Chaguaramas which created a common market and provided machinery for regional co-operation in a number of areas. The supreme authority established by the Treaty is the Heads of Government Conference consisting of the Prime Ministers of the independent and the Premiers of the dependent territories.

The common market has established free trade within the Commonwealth Caribbean and a common external tariff. This has provided for greater industrial development within the member territories. It is significant that there has been a considerable rise in the value of intra-regional trade since 1974.

In the area of functional co-operation, great strides have been made in health, meteorology, transportation, agriculture, university education and foreign policy co-ordination. And great hopes are now being placed on the development of a regional food plan that is designed to satisfy the demands of rising living standards in the Caribbean.

Meeting the Difficulties
Yet the difficulties in the way of reaching the desired goals cannot be ignored. Already the differences that bedevilled all regional experiments in the past have been manifesting themselves again. The claim of the British West Indian Airways to be designated as the regional

air carrier gave rise to sharp controversy. The selection of Barbados as the site of the Caribbean Meteorological Institute and of the Regional Development Bank gave rise to much of the insular feeling of the past. Unhappily familiar, too, was the complaint by some in the Windward and Leeward Islands that they continued to be the poor relations of the bigger territories and that they had nothing to gain, at least in the immediate future, from the institution of a free trade area in the Caribbean.

It is heartening to note however that, when the Caribbean Development Bank was established, a decision was taken by the more developed countries of the area to permit the Bank during the early years of its existence to devote most of its resources to the development of the less developed countries. This has helped to generate greater confidence in the latter territories and to calm their fears that the more developed countries were only interested in exploiting their markets.

Concerted Action

In some respects, one of the happiest auguries for the future is the spirit of co-operation and unity of purpose among the Associated States of the West Indies, more commonly known as the Windward and Leeward Islands.

After the breakdown in the Little Eight negotiations, the Windward and Leeward islands formed their own Council of Ministers' and this continues to function satisfactorily up to the present time. The Council is not a legal entity. It has no charter. It provides a forum for the

Sketch Map showing Membership of Some Caribbean Associations

discussion, on a regional basis, of such problems as seismic research, agricultural research, water improvement and the expansion of airport facilities.

Changes in Government
In September 1976, the Democratic Labour Party, led by Errol Barrow, was defeated in a general election by the

Barbados Labour Party, led by J. M. G. 'Tom' Adams, son of Sir Grantley Adams.

The new government at once introduced stringent measures to meet the economic difficulties arising from the energy crisis of the mid 1970s. And among other things, it addressed itself to the task of developing additional manufacturing industries, intensifying the drive for the development of tourism and placing greater emphasis on the importance of agriculture. Not the least of its declared intentions was to work, as it had done before, to promote the cause of regional co-operation and development.

One of the tragedies of our times was the death of Tom Adams at the age of 53 years. He had perhaps driven himself too hard to improve the financial position of the island and died on March 11, 1985, from cardiac failure.

He strove to promote the idea of West Indian consciousness and West Indian co-operation. The leading part he played in the rescue mission to save Grenada from the tyranny of Marxism will long be remembered.

There are many monuments to his memory. Among these are the new edifice to house the Central Bank of Barbados, which incurred some criticism because of the cost of its construction, and the airport to west coast highway that won universal approval.

Tom Adams was succeeded as Prime Minister by Bernard St. John who tried to carry on the work of his predecessor. But Adams' death seemed to give Errol Barrow the opportunity he was waiting for and in the election of May 1986 he won an overwhelming victory, capturing 24 of the 27 seats in the House of Assembly.

According to some analysts, the causes of such a victory seemed to be the leadership of Errol Barrow, the financial proposals of Dr. Richie Haynes and the 'White Shadows' campaign of Dr. Don Blackman.

Barrow seemed to be convinced that the state of his health would not allow him to enjoy a long tenure of office. With an almost uncanny sense, he publicly proclaimed what was to be the line of succession after his death.

Barrow, like Adams, died of a heart attack on June 1, 1987. And, according to the wish he expressed in the public domain, Erskine Sandiford succeeded him as Prime Minister, with Philip Greaves as Deputy Prime Minister.

The new Central Bank

The new Post Office

The Independence Arch

Hope for the Future

In view of all the circumstances that have been reviewed in this chapter, it is not too much to hope that the peoples of all the territories of the Commonwealth Caribbean will encourage all the regional efforts of the present and take heed from the lessons of our recent history. If the example of the Associated States and the European Economic Community is followed in the wider area of the Caribbean, if there is a spirit of give and take among all the territories concerned, Caricom can become a workable arrangement, bringing benefits to all our peoples.

In view of the foregoing, it may be said that, in spite of difficulties that arise from time to time, West Indians are attempting to improve upon the instruments of regional co-operation. Separation by the sea and island jealousies, that surface at times, are factors that have to be taken into consideration. Yet it seems reasonable to expect that all thoughtful Barbadians and West Indians will continue to cherish the concept of regional co-operation and to aim at the creation of a prosperous economic community in the area.

Further Reading

White Paper on Federal Negotiations, 1962–65.
The Agony of the Eight by Sir Arthur Lewis, 1965.
Eastern Caribbean Common Market Agreement, June 9, 1968.
Address to A.G.M. of Barbados Chamber of Commerce
    by E. W. Barrow, May 22, 1969.
Barbados Comes of Age by F. A. Hoyos, 1987.